Sam Curd's Diary

Sam Curd's Diary

The Diary of
a True Woman

Susan S. Arpad

Ohio University Press
Athens, Ohio   London

Library of Congress Cataloging in Publication Data

Curd, Sam, b. ca. 1835.
   Sam Curd's Diary.

     Bibliography: p.
     1. Curd, Sam, b. ca. 1835.   2. Women—United States—
Biography.   3. Women—United States—History—19th
century.   4. Sex role—United States—History—19th century.
5. Role conflict.   I. Arpad, Susan S., 1937-
II. Title.   III. Title: Diary.
HQ1418.C87   1984   305.4′2′0924   83-22082
ISBN 0-8214-0730-9

Introduction and Notes © Copyright 1984 by Susan S. Arpad.

Printed in the United States of America.

Dedicated to

all of the obedient, nameless women
who tried to be true women
but instead of being rewarded,
were punished by random adversity.

Acknowledgments

I would like to express my gratitude to Nancy Lee, who found Sam Curd's diary in the Bowling Green State University Library Popular Culture Collection; to students, for their comments about the diary; to Mark Tisch, for preliminary historical research in Fulton, Missouri; to student workers and Darinda Harner in the Women's Studies Program office, who typed and retyped the manuscript; and to Monty Arpad, who traveled to Fulton and Columbia, Missouri and learned how to do historical research. I am particularly grateful to my feminist friends for struggling with me in our efforts to find our selves, and to Joe Arpad, who helped do research, encouraged and supported, but never tried to direct.

Introduction

SINCE the beginning of the new women's movement in the 1960's, feminist scholars have noted the general invisibility of women's lives. The study of art and literature has been, overwhelmingly, the study of male artists and male authors. Likewise, the "history of mankind" has been to a great extent just that—the history of men's deeds and experiences. Having realized the bias in our knowledge of the total human experience, historians have been hard at work for the last two decades to recover the record of women's lives, their achievements, and their experiences from historical oblivion.

Because "women's work" was considered unimportant in the grand scope of history, very little published material existed except for the lives of those few extraordinary women who had achieved outstanding success in the man's world of politics, economics, and the arts and sciences. Even these women were treated as aberrations, deviants, or important because of sexual characteristics. For instance, Queen Elizabeth I's most notable characteristic in many histories is her virginity. Carrie Nation, on the other hand, is pictured most frequently as a harridan brandishing an ax. Art criticism of Georgia O'Keefe's paintings usually noted their "sexual" imagery and texture.

The first wave of the new feminist history centered around attempts to reevaluate the careers of women who had achieved some fame or fortune, but whose reputations had suffered because of sex-biased criticism or interpretations. Feminist literary critics pointed out, for instance, that the work of Jane Austen, the Brontë sisters, and others has been denigrated because of the author's sex. Historians turned to writing or rewriting the biographies of important female historical figures who had been ignored previously, or whose lives they felt had been wrongly interpreted. Gerda Lerner has called this first stage "compensatory history" or "contribution history."[1]

1

But since few women have been able to achieve greatness in a masculine-defined world, the revival of the reputations of these "women worthies" was not a complete answer to the problem of the invisibility of women's lives. Most women throughout history have led ordinary lives—as have the majority of men. Although there has been a strong historical bias against the common experience in general, men's experiences have made their way into history books. Exploring, hunting, and fighting Indians have been considered fit subjects for historical research, but until recently, contraception, pregnancy, and childbirth have not. When we read about the westward movement, we read about men hewing trees, building houses, and tilling the land. We rarely read about women doing these tasks or about them cooking and laundering for a family over a campfire, or nursing babies while on the move. In the few instances where a woman's experiences have been examined, usually the result has been a stereotype such as "the madonna of the trail"—the sturdy sunbonneted woman trudging determinedly forward with a baby on one hip and a small child clinging to her skirt.[2] In other words, when women have been included in histories, it has been from a masculine point of view.

To recover women's historical experience, it has been necessary to look at the lives of ordinary women from their own point of view. And in recent years a flurry of books by historians has done just this.[3] From a reading of women's personal documents such as letters, diaries, reminiscences, and oral histories, these historians have attempted to reconstruct women's experiences—what happened to them and what meaning they found in their experiences.

I have used several of these books in college courses and the students have found them to be interesting and informative. But I heard repeated complaints from these students: all of the books give small excerpts from the writings of many women—as if to say there is a common female experience and women's lives can be used to illustrate this common experience. The women chosen were also admirable women, strong women, frequently women who asserted their own individuality against prevailing social norms.[4] The students wanted to read a whole diary to know more about one woman's experience. Not a famous or powerful woman—the diaries of Mary Boykin Chesnut, Alice James, or Anaïs Nin would not do—but an ordinary woman like themselves. I couldn't find one in print. My search finally ended in the spring of

1978 when a librarian friend, rummaging in a box of donated books, discovered the diary of M. Samuella Curd. We knew nothing about where the diary had come from, who the diarist was, or, most distressing, what happened to her after the diary ended. A single reading of the yellowed pages convinced me that this was what my students wanted. Although Sam Curd's life was touched by monumental events, her life was an ordinary one, her concerns probably typical of many women who lived when, where and as she did. Her life illustrates the middle class cultural structures of mid-nineteenth-century America and a single woman's responses to that culture and to the events of her life.

The diary's author is not a famous person; she is not even a wholly admirable person. When I first wrote to a publisher friend, suggesting that she might want to publish the diary, she responded:

> I have read the diary and am quite taken with it. It really has a sense of drama and creates interest at several levels, historical, religious, and feminist—even medical. Having just had a baby, I was intrigued and devastated by her entries concerning Patty.

But two months later she wrote again that she had shared Sam's diary with two campus readers who, while they enjoyed reading the diary, thought that the diarist was not a very "interesting person." They suggested, instead, that the diaries of another woman would be more interesting—an Ohio farm woman who labored prodigiously to feed, clothe, and care for her husband and six children, annually canning 100 quarts of peaches, several hundred glasses of jelly, and 25 gallons of apple butter, listing her recipes and her cleaning schedule, and documenting technological changes in American life. The readers were suggesting that a more "interesting" woman was one who lived a materially productive and physically demanding life. In nineteenth-century America there were many such women, particularly in frontier areas and on farms. Where a subsistence economy predominated, women's physical labor was necessary for the maintenance of the family. Those women who endured the physical hardships and succeeded in raising a family under these conditions of necessity were hallowed in pioneer reminiscences, in statues like the madonna of the trail, and more generally, in an honored American stereotype of the "good, hard working pioneer woman." While they by no means achieved a position of equality with men for their productive efforts, their reminiscences indicate that they frequently found meaning in their work, had pride in their skills and accomplishments, and shared with their husbands a sense of having shaped the future.[5]

By the beginning of the nineteenth century, however, economic and social conditions in America had changed significantly the work roles that were available to many people, particulary effecting a new and growing middle class. Industrialization moved the workplace from the home to the factory, dividing men's and women's labor geographically. Henceforth men would work in "the world" and women, at least of the middle and upper classes, would work in "the home." Men's work in a competitive, capitalistic economy increasingly demanded personal characteristics of energy, aggression, and risk-taking. At the same time, women's work was diminished and devalued by the growth of a consumer market economy. Women increasingly became consumers rather than producers. The divergence of men's and women's physical worlds was followed by changes in socially conceived roles for men and women.

> Though they lived in the same houses, men and women spent their days doing very different things, which required different outlooks—not only different but conflicting, for men's and women's values represented competing social orders. In order to succeed in the new world of commercial capitalism, men had to learn to separate morality and sentiment from self-interest, while women, in legitimizing their own domestic activity, called upon the values of the society that commercial capitalism was engaged in destroying. . . .
> Domesticity, or "femininity," required that a woman have a husband who brought home the rewards of competitive labor and also that she rejected the values such work entailed. The reverse was true for men: "masculinity" required having a "feminine" wife while rejecting "feminine" values.[6]

Middle class women, in the early nineteenth century became "the hostage in the home," according to historian Barbara Welter.[7] She became responsible for maintaining those virtues and ideals that men, contaminated by the materialism and competition of "the world," could no longer pursue. Welter catalogued the four cardinal virtues of the true woman as piety, purity, submissiveness, and domesticity. Although the position on a pedestal that these virtues created was a difficult one for many individual women to maintain, such was the power of this culturally approved role, that women struggled to observe its dictates despite adverse conditions.

Historical research is suggesting, increasingly, that many middle class nineteenth century women experienced conflicts as a result of these starkly different, but rigidly defined sex roles. Carroll Smith-Rosenberg, for instance, has suggested that female hysteria may be viewed as "an alternate role option" for women and as a tactic through which some women resolved domestic stress.[8] Barbara Leslie Epstein has pointed to organized religion and moral reform movements as outlets for women's feelings of protest, resentment, and conflict.[9] Ann Douglas has suggested that most middle class women chose an outlet for these stressful conflicts that was not as forceful or dramatic as hysteria or reform movements. Instead, they became the consumers of mass culture and as the major consumers, they "feminized" it—sentimentalized it:

> Sentimentalism is a complex phenomenon. It asserts that the values a society's activities denies are precisely the ones it cherishes; it attempts to deal with the phenomenon of cultural bifurcation by the manipulation of nostalgia. Sentimentalism provides a way to protest a power to which one has already in part capitulated. It is a form of dragging one's heels.[10]

In a society that defined women as other than "healthy, mature, socially competent adults,"[11] sentimentalism would encourage women to avoid the search for true identity by relying instead on narcissistic wishing that the world was other than it was.[12]

While the "good pioneer woman" of the nineteenth century found her identity through work, for Sam Curd and her sisters then and since, necessary work was not available as a means of resolving the conflicts they experienced. Nor did sentimental literature always offer adequate solace when the conflicts arose out of life-shattering events such as migration or death. In order to better understand women's historical experiences, we need to look beyond the "women worthies," the "good women," and the "madonnas." We need to look at women like Sam Curd.

Sam's diary is interesting in and of itself—in her records of personal daily events, events of national significance, and her attempts to find meaning in these events. But the diary is also disturbing. Throughout the diary there is a profound feeling of dissonance—a conflict between Sam's culturally induced expectations and her experiences that fail in many instances to verify her expectations. At one point Sam wrote:

> I feel so terribly gloomy, this evening came thoughts in connection with the future almost overwhelm one, Oh! that I might become more reconciled to my *fate*. I feel as if I never could, I know it is wrong, I have so many blessings such a good home, kind husband who is never ceasing in his goodness to me, & the best of friends. Oh! that I might have the future in the hands of an all wise Creator, feeling that he will do best for me. All kinds of dark forbodings crowd into my mind this evening. I don't feel as if I could express my feelings to a mortal, and only write to try & find relief. Oh! God help me! (2/22/61)

She should have been happy with her "blessings," but she was not. This explicit outburst is unusual because Sam's ordinary reaction was to hide her negative feelings, even in her diary. More usual was her response of denial, as she wrote of her arrival in Fulton as a new bride:

> It was thus I began to feel truly where I was, and how far I had left home friends away. But I resorted to my usual plan, laughed & talked, to conceal my feelings if nothing more. . . . I felt pretty badly. but I think I concealed it. (7/19/60)

While reading the diary may not be a completely comfortable experience, it is important because the same dissonance that Sam Curd experienced continues to occur in many women's lives when their experiences contradict what their culture has led them to expect. A century after Sam Curd wrote her diary, Betty Friedan describes this same sense of dis-ease in *The Feminine Mystique* as "the crisis in women's identity." Some modern psychologists believe that this dissonance—the unresolved identity crisis—is a major cause of depression in women. Jean Baker Miller writes that, in a sense, "psychological problems are not so much caused by the unconscious as by deprivations of full consciousness."[13] Sam Curd's typical response to conflicts expressed or implied in her diary, was to avoid them, to wish that they were not there. But we do sense that her diary writing is an attempt—however unsuccessful—to come to a fuller consciousness of her identity.

$$* \quad * \quad * \quad * \quad * \quad * \quad * \quad *$$

In an attempt to understand Sam Curd's consciousness of the world and of herself in the world, we can begin by examining her physical circumstances—what a sociologist might identify as her "class": her economic situation, her social connections, and the work that is done to maintain her status. Sam's status derives from two sources: her family of origin in Richmond, Virginia and her family of marriage in Fulton, Missouri.

Sam—Mary Samuella Hart—was the second of four daughters born to Francis Bickley Hart and Martha Jane Dandridge. We don't know much about Martha Dandridge (she was evidently an orphan in 1828 when she married Francis Hart and she died in 1849 or 1850), but we have considerable evidence of Francis Bickley Hart's place in the world. His father was Andrew Hart, who was born in Scotland in 1754, became a successful merchant near Staunton, Virginia; was the owner of a plantation called Sunny Bank and a ruling elder in Cove Church. Andrew married twice, first to Elizabeth Leake and secondly to Elizabeth Bickley; ten children survived to adulthood. (See Appendix A: Hart Family Genealogy.) Some idea of Andrew's economic position can be ascertained from his will. When he died in 1832, Andrew left the following specified items to his wife and children: the 535 acre estate called Sunny Bank, his library, twenty-four slaves, a tract of land in Kentucky, cattle, sheep, and hogs, and $5600. Much of the estate had alreay been distributed, however, for two of the daughters had already married and had received Negroes and money, and the three older sons of the second marriage (James, John, and Francis B.) already had in their possession land, Negroes, horses, and

"Stock of every kind." Francis, for instance, had received a plantation at Covesville—perhaps as a wedding gift in 1828—which he sold in 1837 when he moved to Richmond. The estate inventory valued the twenty-four slaves at $11,026.50, although a codicil to the will provides an interesting insight into the family's existence amidst this seeming plethora of property:

> Whereas I have made ample provision in the body of my will for my three sons James, John, and Francis and whereas considering the number of old slaves which will have to be divided among my 3 daughters and my son Sam likely to prove burdensome to which it is my will that James, John, and Francis shall each take one of the old slaves after the death of my wife and support them during their lives.[14]

Francis Bickley Hart moved to Richmond around 1837, where he set himself up as a "grocer and commission agent."[15] His home, on the northeast corner of Grace and Madison Streets, was in a prosperous residential area, near the Public Square. In the 1840 census, Francis was listed as having in his Richmond household: two white females ages 20-30 (one of whom was probably his wife Martha, the other is unidentified), two white females ages 5-10, (probably Sam and her older sister Jane), and one white female aged under 5 (probably Sam's sister Betty). Five slaves also lived in the household: one female age 24-36, one female age 10-24, one male age 10-24, and two males under age 10. Ten years later, in the 1850 census, the two older women were not listed, and one female named Martha of one year of age is listed. (See Appendix B: 1840 and 1850 census.) Perhaps Sam's mother died after bearing this child. In 1850 Jane was twenty years old. Also living in the household was Matthew G. Anderson, age 27, perhaps the "cousin Matt" in Sam's diary who married "sister." Slaves were not listed as part of the household in 1850. The Richmond Property Tax Book for 1860 lists Francis's personal property as:

	value
2 slaves who have attained the age of 12 years	
1 cattle, sheep, or hog	30
1 watch	50
1 clock	5

	value
1 piano or harp	150
all gold or silver plate or jewelry	100
all household or kitchen furniture	400
capital invested or used in any manufacturing or mining business, for which no license is required	3000
tax	18.14[16]

Francis' property listed for tax purposes changed little during and after the war years (except, of course, that the slaves disappeared), so we can conjecture that his economic status was relatively stable until his death in 1882. He was a merchant involved to some extent in the mercantile life of the city and the surrounding countryside, although his name never appears as an officer or member of Richmond's commercial or civic societies. His status is probably best described as "middling": comfortable, genteel, and stable.

When Sam married Mr. Thomas Curd of Fulton, Missouri, she married a man who was like her father, a merchant whose family connections in Virginia extended back to the eighteenth century. But the Curds, unlike the Harts, had migrated westward in the 1820s and this movement to the western frontier would mark a vast difference between the two families. It is, of course, impossible to say whether the family's entrepreneurial temperament caused the westward migration or whether the opportunities of the sparsely settled frontier elicited an entrepreneurial spirit, but the Curd family history clearly indicates that the male members of both first and second generations in Missouri aggressively pursued a variety of economic, political, and social opportunities to enhance their status.

Tom Curd's father, Dr. Isaac Curd, was born in Goochland, Virginia in 1783; he was one of five surviving children. Isaac's father, John Curd, died in 1819. Among the possessions he named in his will were houses and lands in Goochland and Bedford counties and at least forty-two Negro slaves.[17] Isaac studied medicine at the University of Pennsylvania in Philadelphia. In 1808 he married Jane Watkins. They had ten children, six of whom were living at the time Sam wrote her diary.

In 1824 the family "removed" to Chillicothe, Ohio, where Isaac practiced medicine. Six years later the doctor moved his family to

St. Louis, Missouri and within a year he had moved westward to Callaway County. In addition to practicing medicine in the young town of Fulton, Dr. Isaac Curd was a member of the state legislature, was the first Missouri Bank Examiner, was a delegate to the National Whig Convention, and was an acquaintance of Henry Clay and Thomas H. Benton. In Fulton his business interests included operating a newspaper and acting, for twenty years, as the president of a local bank. Dr. Isaac died in 1850; his wife had died four years earlier. In 1860, when Sam began her diary, her surviving "in laws" were "Kitty" Digges, living in Glasgow, Missouri; John Curd, age 43, unmarried; Isaac Curd, age 34, unmarried; Edwin B. Curd, age 31, unmarried; and Martha Jane ("Matt") Curd, age 27, unmarried. (See Appendix C: Curd Family genealogy.)

A brief sketch of each of Tom Curd's three brothers is perhaps the best way to introduce the family into which Mary Samuella Hart married. John Curd left Fulton, Missouri in 1843 when he was 26 years old, and settled in St. Joseph, Missouri, where he "erected a store on the corner of Levee and Jule streets, the building being at that time the best store in the place."[18] St. Joseph was one of the three major "jumping-off places" on the Missouri River and the Curd store evidently did a large business in supplying the westward-bound migrants moving by horse and wagon across the frontier. John held the positions of City and County Treasurer in St. Joseph city and Buchanan County for many years. He never married; he died in 1865.

Brother Isaac left Fulton in 1842 when he was sixteen years old, and went to Dubuque, Iowa, where he was a clerk in a dry-goods store. In 1849, he moved to St. Joseph and joined brother John in his mercantile business; that business closed in 1861. In later life, a portrait and biographical record of Isaac described his economic and political interests:

> Since 1861 the attention of our subject has been largely given to his real estate interests, which are considerable, as the property has grown remarkably in value. He has owned about fifty acres now comprised within the city limits, and still owns about eighty acres adjoining the city, in addition to other lands in Kansas and elsewhere, having about 800 acres in different farms.
>
> For about seven years he was a Director for the old

Farmers' and Mechanics' Savings Bank, and was also once a Director in the branch of the State Bank of Missouri. He was also an organizer of the old Insurance Company which was established in 1850, and in company with a partner built the brick stores on Felix street now occupied by Henry Brill as a book store, which property he still owns. At one time he was a member of the City Council from the Third Ward. He has assisted in the building of all the railroads centering at this city, among these being the Hannibal & St. Joseph, the St. Joseph & Denver, St. Joseph & Topeka, and also the Narrow Gauge . . .[19]

Isaac, like John never married; he died in 1914.

Brother Ed left Fulton in 1843 at age fourteen for Columbia, Missouri, where he became a clerk in a "business house." Five years later he joined with a group of young men from Callaway County in the gold rush to California, where he remained for three years, "not without some pecuniary profit." In 1852 he returned to Fulton and set himself up as a merchant. In 1866 in St. Louis, he opened a wholesale drug house which burned to the ground at a considerable loss, in 1868. After that time Edwin's business centered in banking and investments. He was a stockholder and the president of the Callaway Savings Bank and had interests in diverse businesses such as the Callaway Lime and Cement Company, Gilbert and Curd Tobacco Co., and Howard Fire Clay Manufacturing Company. He served in city and county public offices, as a director of the State Lunatic Asylum, as a deacon of the First Presbyterian Church, and as a member of the Board of Trustees of Westminster College.[20] In 1865 Edwin married Harriet Webster; they had eight children. He died in 1914.

When Sam Curd moved as a bride from Richmond to Fulton her economic circumstances changed dramatically. In addition to owning and operating the general store called "Curd & Brothers" on Court Street in Fulton, the Curd brothers had set up series of partnerships between themselves and with other individuals to borrow and lend money, to buy and sell land in Callaway and Buchanan Counties, Missouri and Doniphan County, Kansas, to own shares of stock in at least three banks, and to buy and sell farm produce and stock. (See Appendix D: Deeds and Inventories of Thomas Curd's Estate.) But all of this entrepreneurial activity took place outside of Sam's world; she ignored it, recording simply in her diary, "Mr. Curd down town." Only once, when Curd & Brothers partnership was broken up, did she mention anything specific about business: "Today the partnership of Curd & Bro-was dissolved Mr. John Curd selling his portion to Mr. Edwin. Am afraid Bro John is in a rather bad fix for security ship." (10/24/61) Sam's economic status would define, in part, the world in which she lived, but the world of business was clearly not her responsibility.

Sam's "sphere of influence" was the social, rather than the economic world. This world, centering in her home and spreading outward in a carefully nurtured network of relatives, friends, and acquaintances, would engage most of Sam's interest and time. A man's success in the world of business was determined in large part by the property he acquired. Success for a woman was determined in large part by the extent of the social network she could maintain and, interestingly enough, Sam frequently used the commercial language of her husband's world to describe her "business" of socializing. Sam took her business very seriously.

The diary begins, significantly, on the day of Sam's marriage—a watershed event in the life of nineteenth-century women. Before marriage a female operated in the social world created by her parents or other families, where she was cared for and largely care-free. This was particularly true for the antebellum South, where a slave economy helped to create the ideal of the southern belle.[21] In describing her younger unmarried sister, Betty, who was twenty-one years old at the time, Same wrote: "Poor Betty she says she will miss me as much as when I left at first, it is a pity a young girl should have such cares, so much, it makes them prematurely old." (6/22/61) And twice in her diary when she was away from Fulton we catch glimpses of the playful and carefree southern belle that Sam must have been before she was married. At one point on her honeymoon when she and her unmarried sister-in-law Matt were alone, she wrote, "[we] had dinner sent to our rooms charged $2.00 extra, we had a '*heap*' of fun. Dr. L. came almost in the room whilst Matt was undressed, grand scampering." (5/10/60) Later, when she traveled to Boonville she wrote, "Andy, Eliza & myself out to Mr. Hoge's, spent a pleasant day cutting up all sorts of capers. Andy in great glee." (9/28/60)

But when a nineteenth-century woman married she took on

the entire responsibility for creating a social world for her new family. This social world was called, simply, the "home." On the last day of her honeymoon, at Niagra Falls, she and her new husband parted from her paternal family and Sam wrote:

> It was an evening to me of peculiar sadness. We had been together for some days, & this was the eve previous to our sounding the sad word fare-well to those who were dear to me & who had lived with me under the same roof, my dear little sister, for she was much younger than I was. From this time the Scenes & whole Tenor of my life, would change. I would soon turn my face Westward away from the scenes of *home* and childhood, a new sphere of action would open before me, and on me in great measure must depend the making of a *home* happy or miserable, whilst talking & laughing these thoughts would crowd out others, and naturally make me sad. And as the last sound of good night fell on my ears, I could but ask, will we? can we ever meet thus again? and a voice within me whispered, *never!*—(5/15/60)

A close examination of this melodramatic but highly conventional entry in the diary tells us much about Sam Curd's consciousness of the world.

First, is the matter of parting. The opening of the western territories to settlement in the nineteenth century meant that many women would experience these partings as they accompanied husbands and families to new homes. In leaving family and friends they frequently left a close-knit and sheltered circle of female companionship that provided them with emotional support and meaning at every important event of their lives, from birth to death.[22] Julie Roy Jeffrey, in her study of pioneer women's diaries, letters, and reminiscences, notes that women frequently used death images when describing parting scenes, so deep was their sense of loss.[23] So painful was this parting for Sam that her language changed during the passage, from descriptive to melodramatic; she avoided directly confronting the situation by falling back on the highly artificial literary conventions of women's sentimental literature: "And as the last sound of good night fell on my ears, I could but ask, will we? can we ever meet again? and a voice within whispered, *never!*"

Ann Douglas believes that sentimentalism such as this conceals a lack of true purpose:

> Sentimentalism, unlike the modes of genuine sensibility never exists except in tandem with failed political consciousness. A relatively recent phenomenon whose appearance is linked with capitalist development, sentimentalism seeks and offers the distraction of sheer publicity. Sentimentalism is a cluster of ostensibly private feelings which always attains public and conspicuous expression. Privacy functions in the rituals of sentimentalism only for the sake of titillation, as a convention to be violated. Involved as it was with the exhibition and commercialization of the self, sentimentalism cannot exist without an audience.[24]

Sam used the melodramatic here to avoid a true recognition of what was happening in the situation. But the language she used—of finality and death—indicates that she was subconsciously aware of the meaning of the situation. Her old self, the gay southern belle, was expected to die and a new personality, the married woman with her own sphere of action, was expected to emerge. This sphere of action was called the "home," but it included the entire social world that helped to define the family's status.

The family's social status—the network of connections within which much of the family's (particularly the female members') social activities took place—was like its economic status: ample, dependable, and widespread. Beginning with Sam's wedding trip, her life was a progression of visits from one family member or family friend to the next. In Alexandria, Virginia she saw Aunt Julia Hart and cousins Sarah and Henry. In Baltimore she dined with old friends (the Stevensons), and Mr. Dunning paid a visit at their hotel. In Philadelphia Mr. Scott, a Curd family friend paid a call. In New York she visited cousin Eliza Price. At their hotel in Niagara Falls they were visited by a Col. Quarles and Miss McAfee. Wherever she went, there was a familiar face and a familiar protocol for visiting. Sam's social world must have seemed very familiar and comfortable.

The extent and closeness of this network of connections is perhaps the best seen when Sam returned to Richmond for a visit in 1861. Her three-and-a-half-month stay was filled with visits to and from family and old friends. At one point, Sam made an extended journey northwestward from Richmond. The record of her trip gives us a clearer idea of the extent of her family circle. In Goochland County she visited Curd family relatives. In Albermarle County and further west in Staunton she visited her father's relatives, the Harts, and a few of her mother's relatives, the Dandridges. Of the fifty-two people mentioned in the diary by name on this journey, at least twenty-five were closely related to Sam by blood or marriage.

It was this family—the Virginia network—for which Sam was homesick when she moved to Missouri. When she was distressed by problems in Fulton, she wished she could talk to the Virginia family: "Not a word from home; how comforting it would be to be able to pour out my mind into their ears." (3/11/62) Part of her dissatisfaction with the family into which she married was that it had so few members.

> . . . poor Matt is a sore trial to him [Tom Curd]; her brothers have been all in all to her. I wish she would feel to me as a sister. She is as kind as one could be to me, & I miss her so much if away I don't know what I would do without her, I feel so sad [erasure] brother Ed has gone to Jefferson, we have so few in family. (3/15/62)

The divided loyalties she felt and her ambivalence about them were expressed more directly later:

> What would I not give to have my dear father with me, & my other friends; he has always been with me in trouble; but not even a line of comfort from him can I have. . . .
> My own family, I mean Matt & brother Ed, are & do all that kindness can suggest; but it is natural for us to feel a yearning for those who have been with us from infancy. I don't know what I would do without Matt she is all a sister could be. (4/1/62)

This is not to say that Sam's paternal family was restricted to Virginia; to the contrary, the family network extended even to Missouri. In fact, Sam's marriage to Tom Curd was not the first Hart/Curd marital alliance. Andrew Hart's first wife (Elizabeth

Leake) had borne a son, Samuel Frances Leake Hart, who married
Ann Taylor Curd and moved to Fulton, Missouri. When Sam
moved to Fulton, one of the first visits she paid was to this old
"Aunt Ann." In addition, of the families Sam visited when she arrived in Fulton, she was directly related to the Dyers, the Hockadays, the Tuttles, the Lawthers, the Wells, the Abbotts, and the
Nicholsons. It was probably on a visit to these Fulton relatives two
years earlier that Sam had met Thomas Curd.

Although the Curd family network in Missouri was not as extensive as Sam's Virginia network, part of Sam's "job" in creating a
home and family in Missouri was to "visit," and thus to extend the
family's social network. When she first arrived in Fulton, "for
some time, my time was taken up receiving and paying calls." The
visits were highly ritualized and most etiquette books of the period contained separate sections on visiting, including the proper
use of calling cards, correct visiting hours, the hierarchy of who
could call upon whom, and personal manners while calling. The
importance and meaning of visiting were described in one such
book as:

> Such visits are necessary, in order to maintain good feeling
> between the members of society; they are required by the
> custom of the age in which we live, and must be carefully
> attended to.

and

> The chain which binds society together is formed of innu-
> merable links. Let it be your part to keep those links uni-
> formly bright; and to see that neither dust nor rust accumu-
> late upon them.[25]

Although the degree of formality varied with the intimacy of the
acquaintanceship, visits between even the most intimate of
friends were mentally logged in as debits or credits.

Visiting became, for many middle class women of the mid-
nineteenth century, a "business" of maintaining the family's social
network and the language used to describe the activity was commercial. After Sam's confinement for childbirth, she wrote that
she was in "arrears" and so made many short visits to balance her

accounts. The visits made each day were carefully entered in her diary/ledger. (An interesting sidelight to Sam's manuscript diary is that it was written in an account book.) When Sam visited the Misses Hockaday, the latter "insisted on our staying all day, & said they would not call it a visit until we did come so." In other words, the visit would not "count" if not sufficiently long.

Part of the social networking was carried out under the guise of religion—prayer meetings, teaching Sunday School, cleaning and decorating the church, revival meetings, and entertaining the minister. Church activities were some of the few active roles that middle class nineteenth-century women could take. Since the early years of the century Sunday School teaching had been a particularly popular active role for evangelical young women. It offered them the companionship of like-minded teachers and scholars and it provided one of the few acceptable outlets for their aggressive energies in recruiting, organizing, and teaching their classes.[26] Teaching Sunday School was discussed by Sam with the same commercial imagery as visiting. She "accumulated" scholars for her class, always giving the number in attendance, but rarely mentioning the content of the lesson. At revival meetings the numbers of converts were always given, as they were at prayer meetings.

Women's attendance in churches was markedly greater than men's during the nineteenth century. While some historians believe this difference was more pronounced after the Second Great Awakening, Ann Douglas argues that men's church attendance was always small. However, during the nineteenth century women's "influence" in the church increased; piety and theology became "feminized"—less theological and more sentimental. As the divisions between men's world of business and public life and women's sphere of home and church increased, men appeared more "ungodly" than ever and women appeared to be more moral and religious.[27] Barbara Leslie Epstein suggests that the stark division of sex roles in the nineteenth century created an antagonism between the sexes that frequently was expressed in religious terms.

Women often regarded revivals, and especially the conversions of formerly irreligious men, as victories, though they were careful to point out that in scoring such triumphs they

were acting only as the agents of Christ and not for themselves. In many families revivalism became a focus of conflict,
in which were at stake not only divergent religious convic-
tions but also a woman's relative power in the family. . . .[28]

Although this antagonism was never expressed directly, we find
evidence of it in Sam's diary when she worried about her husband's "ungodliness" and finally, triumphantly, achieved his "public profession of religion."
    Sam's diary certainly gives evidence that she considered herself
a success in her roles as religious person and as creator and main-
tainor of a social network outside of the "home". Oddly enough,
the home itself—what we would expect to be the center of Sam's
life and attention—received very little commentary in the diary.
We can only speculate on the reasons for the omission. Certainly,
there is a human tendency in storytelling to focus on the extraordinary and to assume that the ordinary and the habitual need
not be discussed.[29] But in Sam's case there seem to be other reasons why she neglected discussing her home. The first is that
when she came to Fulton as a new bride, Sam, her husband Tom,
her sister-in-law Matt, and other assorted relatives and business
relations moved into a home run by Mrs. Mary A. McKinney.
"Boarding out" was a common experience in nineteenth-century
America, particularly for unmarried people and for married cou-
ples without children, especially in a frontier area where housing
was likely to be in short supply.[30] During their first year of marriage Tom and Sam began building their own home about three
city blocks from Mrs. McKinney's house. They moved to this new
house shortly before their first child was born. But even for this
house there is almost no description in the diary. (See Appendix D:
Inventory of Tom Curd's Estate: Household Goods, for an account
of the rooms and furnishings of Sam's house.)
    Likewise, there is little mention in the diary of work that Sam
did in the home. Frequently she wrote, "The day passed in the
normal order of things." or, "All things occurred in the usual routine." But there is little specific detail about that routine. Several
times she mentioned reading: "did my usual reading in the morning." We suspect that this reading was largely religious in nature.
Sam mentioned reading Alexander's Christian Experience and she
wrote several times about "improving the day" by her reading.

The single most frequently mentioned type of work was sewing: of the sixty notations in the diary of specific work, thirty involved some kind of sewing. She noted the making of pillowcases and quilts, the making of ottomans for the new house, and sewing for soldiers, but most of the sewing involved making and remaking clothes for herself and other women. In addition, there are eight mentions of canning and preserving, including peach preserves, damson preserves, tomato "pikle," calves feet jelly, "green pickle," drying "the lard of two hogs," and smoking meat.

Sam mentioned some other food preparation experiences, but each time it was to record a disaster:

> Helped Matt make cake for party. All discouraged at the complete failure in baking. (8/23/60) tried some more cake, a total failure again. (8/24/60)

> Made an attempt to make Molasses Candy—after wasting our strength out—it turned to molasses. (1/14/61)

> Had quite an accident happen to the custard, there was a leak in the freezer & just as it was doing finely discovered that there was more salt coming in than was palatable, and the whole thing was spoiled, opened some peaches for substitute (10/19/61)

> Had quite an amusing time at dinner. There was the toughest kind of chicken so much so that everybody nearly, left the original piece on his or her plate; and the cream was so poor, that I felt the credit of the family was below par for palateable dinners. (10/24/61)

Other than sewing and food preparation, housework was rarely mentioned. The heavier labor of maintaining a household was almost entirely ignored: housecleaning was mentioned once, laundry, never.

We suspect the chief reason for this omission was that someone else was doing the household labor—someone whose presence was assumed but not worthy of note—slaves. The matter of slaves is problematic. We know from a brief comment about her visit to a Woman Suffrage Convention in New York that Sam strongly disapproved of mixed racial seating. "I was shocked to see negro men and women take seats in the white congregation but nothing is too disgusting for them." (5/10/60) Except for this mention, however, slaves and the issue of slavery are absent from the diary. There is a great deal of external evidence, however, pointing to the probability that there were slaves in Sam's Fulton household.

Missouri was a slaveholding state in 1860, and both the Hart and Curd families had been slaveowners.[31] Callaway County was one of three counties in Missouri known as "Little Dixie" because of the predominantly southern origins of its early settlers. The slave census of 1860 indicates that at least several of the families close to the Curds owned slaves. For instance, Hans Lawther (cousin Virginia's husband) owned ten slaves in three slave houses, Sam Dyer owned three, Robert Dyer owned two, and W. W. Tuttle (cousin Sue's husband) owned eight. In the Probate Court records of Thomas Curd's estate there appears a year's contract to hire a slave:

> On or before the first day of January 1862 we promise to pay Jesse Glover one hundred and ninety dollars for the hire of his yellow man [here the world "Rafe" has been inserted above the line with a caret] for the year 1861. We are to cloth said Rafe and Glover is to pay his Doctor bill and taxes. January 1st 1861. (Signed) Curd & Bros.

This must be the "Ralfe" mentioned in Sam's diary (1/1/62) when Tom Curd was unable to hire him the following year.[32] Finally, the inventory of Tom Curd's household goods suggest that there was a room or rooms beyond the kitchen, perhaps in a separate building, containing "1 Bed Stead & Beding, lounge & Beding, 1 Ward robe & Bureau, Carpet & stools, 1 Rocking & 5 chairs, 2 Curtains" in which slaves were probably lodged. (See Appendix D).

One other incident gives us a hint that Sam purposefully ignored slaves in her diary. In the autumn of 1860 Sam took a trip to Boonville and Columbia to visit friends and to attend the Presbyterian synod meeting. While she was absent from Fulton a white woman was brutally murdered by an "impudent and insolent" female slave. The story as told in the *Missouri Telegraph* of October 2, 1860, contained most of the details of the slaveowner's most fearful nightmare:

On Saturday last one of the most cold-blooded and cruel murders was perpetrated, on the person of Miss Susan Jemima Barnes, that it has ever been our misfortune to chronicle. All of the white persons belonging to the house were gone to church, some two miles distant, and the negro woman was sent into the field to work. Miss Barnes lived about eight miles east of this city, with her brother and mother.

Some time during the day, perhaps about twelve o'clock (as Miss Barnes had already prepared dinner,) she was most inhumanly butchered. It seems that she was sitting in the kitchen knitting at the time she was first attacked. Between the kitchen and the east room of the dwelling there is a small passage through which Miss Barnes fled and passed into the east room. There she was also attacked, either with a shovel or a pair of heavy iron tongs. The shovel handle was very much bent, and was straight in the morning.

From the east room she passed to the west, leaving a strand of yarn, with which she was knitting, behind her. In the west room she was overpowered, knocked down, and her head so beaten and broken that not a whole bone remained, except the right cheek bone, which gave no indication of being fractured. Her brains were scattered over the floor, a large pool of blood under her head, and every indication of a terrible struggle having taken place between her and the murderer. There were the marks of bloody hands on the wall, blood on everything about the house, and an evidence that, in all probability, a knife had been used at some time during the difficulty, as Miss Barnes' hand was very much cut.

A mob of forty to fifty "exasperated" men took the negro, named Teney, from the deputy constable who was taking her to Fulton, and hung her from a tree.[33] Certainly, Sam must have heard or read the stories on her return a few days later to Fulton, but the incident was not mentioned in the diary.

In 1860 the subject of slavery was the single most important topic of national debate. It was argued from the point of view of morality and religion as well as society, family and economics; debates were carried on in the press as well as in the home. Missouri was one of the "new" states about which the issue of the legality of slaveholding had been most heatedly debated. That the issue was entirely ignored in the diary says a great deal about Sam Curd's consciousness of the world in which she lived. In avoiding the mention of individual slaves or the issue of slavery, she avoided the tensions and conflicts that a discussion of slavery entailed. If we assume that one of the purposes of diary writing is to "create a world according to our own wishes,"[34] we realize that Sam Curd created in her diary a world in which problematic issues other than her own personal concerns, did not exist.

One other area of Sam's physical context at home needs to be mentioned—her attitude toward motherhood and children. As we have seen, Sam began the diary with a strong resolve to create a happy "home," which in the didactic domestic literature of the period, was assumed to include children. And within sixteen months of her wedding, Sam gave birth to a child. But the evidence of the diary strongly suggests that Sam's attitude toward children was ambivalent. She approved of motherhood in principle, but several times in the diary she expressed pity for women who had several small children. For instance, when visiting in Virginia, Sam wrote, "Mary Dowden had a boy last night, her next youngest only *13 months* old, she is to be pitied." (6/3/61) Sam also noted an implied connection between a woman's ill health and her many children: ". . . from there to Lizzie Morton's, found the latter quite unwell, has an infant, little girl, about 4 weeks old, this is her 5th child, it seems most impossible spent some time with her . . ." (4/11/61) So pronounced was Sam's conviction that repeated childbirth and ill health were linked that she didn't seem to notice the contradiction when she wrote about another woman, "cousin A has three babies, it is such a charge for so delicate a person, her health is better than usual." (3/28/61) The high birth rate in the nineteenth century was due to several factors, including insufficient knowledge of birth control methods and an emphasis on the role of women as mothers. During the nineteenth century, however, the birth rate for white women in the United States was declining dramatically. According to Carl Degler, fertility declined by fifty percent between 1800 and 1900.[35] Sam's attitude toward frequent childbirth seems to reflect this new situation.

The diary suggests, further, that Sam may not have even liked being with children and that she did not experience mothering as an entirely fulfilling job. For instance, when Sam lived in Mrs. McKinney's house in Fulton, there were three McKinney children (ages nine to eighteen) living in the house, but they were never mentioned in the diary during the first seven months, and then only to note on Christmas day that "the children were up looking after their stockings." In fact, until she had her own child, Sam usually mentioned children only when they were sick or dying. Her diary presents considerable evidence that Sam did not feel a great mothering instinct even after she became a mother. She admired other women's devotion to babies and frequently wished that she were a better mother. A month after Patty's birth, she wrote, "Miss Lizzie came and nursed the baby a little while. She seems so devoted to babies, I wish I had her tact and love for them." (9/23/61) Sam noted baby Patty's growth and charm, but at the same time we read resentment that she was no longer free to "go out". We can almost hear Sam's sigh as she wrote, "Intended going to church but the baby had the colic until it was too late, a little baby takes up a great deal of time." (10/6/61)

One indication of Sam's distance from the child was her reticence to call the baby by name. Named "Adele May" at birth, the baby was christened "Martha Hart" more than three months later because "the men were so opposed to fancy names." But Sam continued to call her "the baby" in the diary until she was six and a half months old, and then she was called "Patty Curd." Sam's feelings of distance from the baby were, perhaps, in part the result of her fear that the baby might die. Children's deaths were an ever-present reality in nineteenth century life. During the first five months described in Sam's diary, she mentioned the deaths of at least eight of the children of her friends, not counting miscarriages and still births. At one point in the diary Sam indicated that if she loved the baby too much, she might be punished by the baby's death: "The baby has a bad cold it distresses to hear her cough am afraid some thing will happen of it. I trust not to cling too much to her, for we are not permitted to make ourselves idols & keep them." (2/28/62) Although she hesitated to love her baby too much for fear it would die, at another point late in the diary she wrote:

> . . . but for the great interest in my darling Patty, I should be undone. She is the source of greatest comfort to me, talk-

ing now, and as bright and winning in her ways as she can be.
God has been merciful to spare her, may her life be precious
in his sight. (6/15/63)

The subjects of death, in particular, and religion, in general, are
the most evident unresolved—even unexamined—dissonances in
Sam Curd's life.

On her honeymoon, Sam visited several cemeteries. In Philadelphia, "Went to Laural Hill Cemetery. This is a lovely spot, some
very handsome Tomb Stones, have a fine view of the Schuylkill
from several points." (5/8/60) In New York:

> Matt, Mr. Curd & myself, went to Green Wood Cemetery.
> Went over in the omnibus & horse car, got a hack after get-
> ting there & rode over the grounds. it is truly an enchanting
> spot, Nature & Art have contributed largely to its beauty.
> Many of the Tomb Stones are splendid & the view of the bay
> from many points is very fine. (5/11/60)

Taking a holiday excursion to the cemetery had become a popular
diversion in the mid-nineteenth century. Ann Douglas' description of the "rural cemetery movement" and her analysis of the
attendant "domestication of death" accurately describe Sam
Curd's mind-set here about death:

> By the 1830's . . . the intramural churchyard was replaced
> by the landscaped "garden" or "rural" cemetery, located
> away from the church on the outskirts of town or vil-
> lage. . . . The new, planned, and picturesque rural cemeter-
> ies, unlike their intramural predecessors, were dedicated to
> the idea that the living, and dead, still "cared." Paths with
> pastoral names, gentle rills, green slopes, and newly popular
> graveside flowers flattered the presumed docility of the de-
> ceased. . . . It is not so much that the dead are alive as they
> they are altogether accessible to the living. . . .
> Nothing speaks more clearly to the transformation of
> death the rural cemeteries promulgated than their promo-
> tion as places of resort, well suited to holiday excur-
> sions. . . . The mid-nineteenth-century American went to

the cemetery rather in the spirit in which his twentieth-century descendant goes to the movies: with the hopefulness attendant upon the prospect of borrowed emotions. The rural cemetery's camouflage of death was so entire that its purpose came paradoxically to seem the creation of the *illusion* of death for the vicarious edification and stimulation of the living. The cemetery functioned not like experience but like literature; it was in several senses a sentimental reader's paradise.[36]

This same domestication of death is evident in the mourning poems that Sam copied so painstakingly in the back of her diary. And, at times, she viewed the real or impending deaths of friends with this same sentimentalized attitude. When she received a letter about her cousin Betsy Dew's death in Virginia, Sam wrote in her diary:

"oh! how mysterious are the ways of Providence, we have here verified the fact—Death loves a shining mark, truly a bright star has gone out in, from the circle of her acquaintances & relations. Many there will be to drop a tear of sympathy over her grave. Oh! that the living might improve by these repeated warnings." (8/13/60)

In the puritan tradition, Sam saw death as a lesson for the living— a reminder that life should be a preparation for and an anticipation of death and that the living should emulate the exemplary lives being eulogized.[37] But as David Stannard has pointed out, Americans have always had a profound ambivalence in their feelings about death. In the nineteenth century their religion taught them to long for death as a glorious union with God, but they sentimentalized the mourning process, maintaining a pretence that the dead and the living were still joined.[38]

Sam Curd's reactions to death varied greatly. At times she treated it matter-of-factly: "Lou Cordell's child died at 12 o'clock, went there directly after dinner. Looked so natural. Lou had a great deal of fortitude." (8/16/60) At others, she expressed a conventional puritanical, almost manichean belief in death as a release from pain: "the baby grew worse until 2 o'clock when it exchanged the pains of this life, for one of eternal Bliss." (8/13/60) But at other times, particularly when she noted women as mourners, she emphasized the pain of bereavement:

> News came before the service was taken that Dr. Overton was dead, died a most triumphant death. But oh! how melancholly the cause. Mrs. O. seems entirely overcome this is her first trouble, poor women it came like a thunderbolt. Oh! the anguish which this has caused. (2/16/62)

When Tom Curd became sick, Sam exhibited the same tension of conflicting belief:

> Mr. C very feeble this evening; it is distressing to see a *man* thus stricken by disease. I trust he has an enduring one & if God should thus afflict me by taking him, I feel he will be prepared, I pray he may have brighter manifestations of his love and forgiveness. Oh! God may he be *spared* for great usefulness. (2/26/62)

Sam's conflicting feelings about death were reflected in her beliefs about religion. Most frequently Sam espoused a belief that God freely worked his providence in the world for the good of humankind. For instance, when she described a drought in Missouri, she ended with a conventional assurance of God's beneficence:

> The whole month of July has been excessively hot & dry for four weeks & more not enough rain fall to wet the ground an inch, vegetation parched & the cry for eatibles & water, with the worst cry of starvation has been sounded. But God reigneth & will not forsake us all together in witholding the latter rain. (7/30/60)

Sam believed that God particularly helped the just, which in the Civil War was the Confederate side. After witnessing a military parade in Richmond, she wrote: "It is truly a sight, but one that makes my heart bleed to see such preparation for killing people. Believing we are in the right, I trust we shall be blessed." (5/17/61) After the Confederate victory at Bethel Church, she noted, "What signal display of the working of Providence that each heart might recognize it." (6/10/61)

This belief in a God who actively worked in the world for good allowed Sam to use God as a way of avoiding the real conflicts in her own life. When she was troubled or in doubt, especially when she experienced conflicts in her beliefs, she appealed to God's wisdom and mercy and then ignored the problem. For instance, at the end of her visit to Virginia, Sam wished to stay there but Tom Curd insisted on returning to Missouri:

> Oh! I wish it suited Mr. C to stay in VA, the dear spot & these such times I feel like all being together but I trust I shall be sustained by an Almighty Arm. Father is very uneasy about my going back, is afraid we will have trouble by the way, & then not be safe after getting there. It is such bad times to say good bye to them all, when we will again meet, God only knows. (6/22/61)

She was distressed by the war, but avoided thinking about it by dismissing it to God:

> The whole land in distress, nothing but awful forebodings of the future. The South arrayed in deadly conflict against the North Oh! distressing! . . .
> Day passes off quickly, one would never imagine that war was going on in the land, from the quietude which reigns. God in his mercy keep us thus through the whole course of events; how long it may be the case, I cant say. but I try to feel, "sufficient unto the day is the evil thereof." (7/4&5/61)

When Mr. Curd became ill, she responded with depression. Unable to take control over her life and her feelings, Sam relied on God to sustain and direct her:

> Am feeling very much depressed Mr. C had night sweats last night, & is very feeble to-day. Oh! I feel as if my heart would sink within me, when I see him look so badly. I am afraid he is prey to consumption. God in mercy spare him, & make him thine own. No tidings from home this makes me unhappy; heard that Mrs. Price was dead, & the moment I wondered

how is father. Oh! What dark days trouble on every hand.
God help me! (1/30/62)

Finally, her faith could not provide her with the solace she sought.
The conflicts between her belief system and her experience of the
world overwhelmed Sam Curd. She had accepted her culture's definition of her self as weak, passive, domestic, and religious; this
acceptance made it impossible for her to even imagine a self in
contradiction to the culture's definition, much less to assert such a
self. Ironically, when crises occurred, the cultural definition of her
self was inadequate to meet and overcome her new circumstances.

*   *   *   *   *   *

The first wave of feminist history was "contribution history,"
in which the lives and works of "great" women were rewritten and
reevaluated. It is an important kind of history because it provides
us with heroic female role models; it celebrates the heroic lives of
individual women who succeeded in a patriarchal world.[39] Contribution history is inadequate by itself because it ignores the lives of
the vast majority of women, whose lives have not been heroic according to the patriarchal model.

The second wave of feminist history could be called "oppression" history. It documented, by looking at popular culture, pre-
scriptive literature, and statistical data about women's lives, the
ways in which women have been oppressed in patriarchal societies.[40] Unsatisfied with this treatment of women as objects, some
oppression historians explored ways in which women responded
creatively to the oppressive circumstances of their lives by maintaining a separate women's culture.[41] This examination and reeval-
uation of women's culture has allowed us to celebrate the positive
aspects of women's lives such as women's friendship networks,
women's arts and aesthetics, and women's perspectives on subjects like religion, politics, and economics.

In many of the recent writings on women's history, historians
have tended to look at "the best" in women's lives, which has been
defined in various ways. We have rewritten the lives of deviant
women like Elizabeth Cady Stanton and Margaret Sanger, who
attempted to redefine themselves and the world from a woman-
centered perspective. We have published biographies of women

like Maria Edgeworth and Catharine Beecher, who accepted an androcentric definition of woman and the world and who achieved popular acclaim in their own times. The current popularity of frontier women as a topic of historical study is, I suspect, in part because the circumstances of subsistence living gave their lives a heroism of hardship endured.[42] Even recent efforts to research what is being called "women's nontraditional literature" frequently has tended to look for secret feminists or unknown literary greats.[43]

Our efforts to celebrate women's lives have led us to question the fundamental value systems by which our culture has decided what is great, good, or beautiful. Why, for instance, are "domestic" arts such as quilting considered less valuable than "fine" arts such as sculpture? Why is war more carefully studied than peacemaking and cooperative living? Why is logical, sequential thinking more valued than intuitive, wholistic thinking? One of the positive consequences of such women's culture studies will undoubtedly be a re-vision of our social construction of reality.

But one of the negative consequences of many "women's culture" studies has been a tendency to look at the female world in isolation, particularly to ignore its relationship to the male world of political and economic power.[44] Most starkly stated, that relationship is one of oppression. Feminist scholars who have studied women as an oppressed group have experienced a dilemma of loyalty. As mentioned above, we have resisted studying women as objects of forces over which they, for the most part, had little control; we have preferred instead to emphasize women's attempts to control and give positive meaning to that world. More difficult, is the negative portrayal of women. In studying them as the victims of oppression, we must show women as damaged and limited human beings. As Sheila Rowbotham noted, "The act of oppression not only disfigures the oppressor, it also maims the oppressed."[45]

In one of the most daring and comprehensive feminist scholarly historical studies of the past decade, Ann Douglas wrestled with this dilemma:

The case of the women is equally painful, but more difficult to discuss, especially in the atmosphere of controversy that attends feminist argument today. I must add a personal note here. As I researched and wrote this book, I experienced a confusion which perhaps other women scholars have felt in recent years. I expected to find my fathers and my mothers; instead I discovered my fathers and my sisters. The best of the men had access to solutions, and occasionally inspiring ones, which I appropriate only with the anxiety and effort that attend genuine aspiration. The problems of the women correspond to mine with a frightening accuracy that seems to set us outside the process of history; the answers of even the finest of them were often mine, and sometimes largely unacceptable to me. I am tempted to account my response socialization, if not treachery. Siding with the enemy. But I think that is wrong.

I have a respect for so-called "toughness," not as good in itself, not isolated and reified as it so often is in male-dominated cultures, but as the necessary preservative for all virtues, even those of gentleness and generosity. My respect is deeply ingrained; my commitment to feminism requires that I explore it, not that I abjure it. Much more important, it does no good to shirk the fact that nineteenth-century American society tried to damage women like Harriet Beecher Stowe—and succeeded. It is undeniable that the oppressed preserved, and were intended to preserve, crucial values threatened in the larger culture. But it is equally true that no one would protest oppression with fervor or justification if it did not in part accomplish its object: the curtailment of the possibilities of growth for significant portions of a given community. Nineteenth-century American women were oppressed, and damaged; inevitably the influence they exerted in turn on their society was not altogether beneficial. The cruelest aspect of the process of oppression is the logic by which it forces its objects to be oppressive in turn, to do the dirty work of their society in several senses. Melville put the matter well: weakness, or even "depravity in the oppressed is no apology for the oppressor; but rather an additional stigma to him, as being, in a large degree, the effect and not the cause of oppression." To view the victims of oppression simply as martyrs and heroes, however, undeniably heroic and martyred as they often were, is only to perpetuate the sentimental heresy I am attempting to study here.[46]

The response of some feminist historians to Douglas' work has been to brand her a traitor.[47]

It is with some feelings of ambivalence that Sam Curd's diary is presented. Sam Curd was not a woman who maintained a critical perspective on her culture; to the contrary, she accepted the role of "true womanhood" and attempted to conform her life to its dictates. Neither was she a woman who found an arena for the satisfying expression of creativity and love within a women's culture; although Sam participated in the ritual of visiting among her circle of women friends, her lack of ego development allowed her little deep empathy for others. Sam Curd is the woman in history we do not want to recognize because it is painful to see ourselves reflected in her—insofar as we have been successfully enculturated, we share Sam's life and fate. She is, as Ann Douglas suggested, our sister.

* * * * *

Sam Curd's diary is presented here in a form as close to the original as possible. Spelling, punctuation, capitalization, and grammar have not been changed except in a few cases. The original is a standard account book, the pages lined horizontally and vertically. The covers are pasteboard. It measures 11 3/4 inches by 7 1/4 inches. The inside front cover contains numerous ink blots and scratch marks—as if someone were testing a recalcitrant pen there—and two inscriptions: "Creosote in water good for swollen feet 5 drops to half bucket" and "M. D. Whiteside/Franklin Kty/ send 15CTS." The diary begins on the first lined page, carefully written in brown ink.

Mr S Curd's Diary Commencing 3rd May

May 3rd On the evening of this day, the marriage ceremony of Mr Thomas S Cura, of Fulton Mo, and myself was performed, by Rev Charles H Reid, of Richmond Va. I had 8 Brides-maids & grooms-men. vij. Misses Dandridge, Betty & Mag Hart, F & J Anderson, E George Mate Curd, & Mr Brooks. Messrs Isaac Curd, John Curd, W Tucker, J Cany, & Anderson's. none but neighbors & attendants present. Directly after the ceremony, we took supper, & left within an hour for Washington. there were nine in party. Fanny Gaines & Mr Seaton Insley, of Hanover Va, who were married the night before. Miss Mate Curd, Betty Hart, Mr John Curd, Mr Wm Tucker, Mr Insley Mr Thomas Curd & myself made up the party. Traveled all night, arrived in Washington just at light, stopped at Brown's Hotel. May 4th Part the party spent the day sight seeing, I was not well enough to go out. May 5th Mr Cura & myself went to Alexandria to see aunt Judia Hart, while the others went sight seeing. Cousin Sarah & Henry came while we were gone, got back too late dinner & started off soon after for Baltimore amidst the shouts of the friends at the Hotel. arrived in Baltimore just before dark, went up to Mr Stevenson's after tea, had fun passing myself off to an old friend as Miss Hart stopped at the Eutaw House. May 6th Spent the Sabbath in Balt. some went to church, I staid with Mate Curd, who was sick, until after service, when Mr Stevenson came for us took me to his house to dine, spent the evening talking over old times with Anna. Mr C came for me took 8 o'clock did not go to church that night Mr Dunning came to see us at the Eutaw House

Notes

1. Lerner, "Placing Women in History: Definitions and Challenges," *Feminist Studies*, III, 1/2 (Fall 1975).

2. See Glenda Riley, *Frontierswoman: The Iowa Experience* (Ames: The Iowa State University Press, 1981) for an extended critique of these stereotypes of pioneer women.

3. See, for instance, Nancy F. Cott, *The Bonds of Womanhood: "Woman's Sphere" in New England, 1780-1835* (New Haven: Yale University Press, 1977); Barbara Leslie Epstein, *The Politics of Domesticity: Women, Evangelism, and Temperance in Nineteenth-Century America* (Middletown, Conn.: Wesleyan University Press, 1981); John Mack Faragher, *Women and Men on the Overland Trail* (New Haven: Yale University Press, 1979); Christiane Fischer, *Let Them Speak for Themselves: Women in The American West, 1849-1900* (New York: E. P. Dutton, 1978); Elizabeth Hampsten, *Read This Only to Yourself: The Private Writings of Midwestern Women, 1880-1910* (Bloomington: Indiana University Press, 1982); Julie Roy Jeffrey, *Frontier Women: The Trans-Mississippi West 1840-1880* (New York: Hill and Wang, 1979); Kathy Kahn, *Hillbilly Women* (New York: Avon Books, 1972); Mary Jane Moffat and Charlotte Painter (eds.), *Revelations: Diaries of Women* (New York: Vintage Books, 1975); Glenda Riley, *Frontierswoman*; Lillian Schlissel, *Women's Diaries of the Westward Journey* (New York: Schocken Books, 1982); Nancy Seifer, *Nobody Speaks for Me!: Self-Portraits of American Working Class Women* (New York: Simon and Schuster, 1976); and Joanna L. Stratton, *Pioneer Women: Voices from the Kansas Frontier* (New York: Simon and Schuster, 1981).

4. Moffat and Painter wrote in introducing *Revelations*, p. 4, "Our own tastes led us to put aside those that posited a self we didn't like or find interesting, and to seek out those that demonstrated character as the ability to make moral distinctions and choices according to a personal code rather than the social or religious codes of the age in which they wrote."

5. John Mack Faragher's recent research on midwestern and pioneering women contradicts earlier, rosier claims that pioneering created sex equity or even androgyny. See, especially, his *Women and Men on the Overland Trail.*

6. Epstein, *The Politics of Domesticity*, p. 62.

7. Welter began one of the earliest studies of the creation of the image of "true womanhood":

> "The nineteenth century man was a busy builder of bridges and railroads, at work long hours in a materialistic society. The religious values of his forebears were neglected in practice if not in intent, and he occasionally felt some guilt that he had turned this new land, this temple of the chosen people, into one vast countinghouse. But he could salve his conscience by reflecting that he had left behind a hostage, not only to fortune, but to all the values which he held so dear and treated so lightly. Woman, in the cult of True Womanhood presented by the women's magazines, gift annuals and religious literature of the nineteenth century, was the hostage in the home."

See "The Cult of True Womanhood: 1820-1860," *American Quarterly* 18 (Summer 1966), 151-174.

8. Smith-Rosenberg, "The Hysterical Woman: Sex Roles and Role Conflict in Nineteenth Century America," *Social Research* 39, 1 (Spring 1972), 652-678.

9. Epstein, *The Politics of Domesticity*. See also, Carroll Smith-Rosenberg, "Beauty, the Beast and the Militant Woman: A Case Study in Sex Roles and Social Stress in Jacksonian America," *American Quarterly*, XXIII, 4 (October 1971), 562-584.

10. Douglas, *The Feminization of American Culture* (New York: Avon Books, 1977), pp. 11-12.

11. See Inge Broverman, Donald Broverman, et al., "Sex-Role Stereotypes and Clinical Judgments of Mental Health," *Journal of Consulting and Clinical Psychology*, 34, 1 (1970), 1-7 and Phyllis Chesler, *Women & Madness* (New York: Avon Books, 1972).

12. Ann Douglas explains this process at one point as:

> "Most simply, one might say that society forces members of a subculture at any moment of intersection with the larger culture into a constant, simplified, and often demeaning pro-

cess of self-identification. . . . Naturally those belonging
to a subculture . . . will struggle obsessively, repetitiously,
and monotonously to deal with the burden of self-dislike implied and imposed by their society's apparently low evaluation of them. In a sense, they will be forced into some version
of narcissism. . . . Narcissism is best defined not as exag-
gerated self-esteem but as a refusal to judge the self by alien,
objective means, a willed inability to allow the world to play
its customary role in the business of self-evaluation. . . .
The narcissist must always by definition be self-taught, because the world's lessons are inevitably unacceptable to his
ego. He is committed not only to an underestimation of the
force of facts, but, in Freud's words, to an "over-estimation
of the power of wishes and mental processes . . . a belief in
the magical virtue of words and a method of dealing with the
outer world—the art of magic."

The Feminization of American Culture, pp. 419-420.

13. Miller, *Toward A New Psychology of Women* (Boston: Beacon
Press, 1976), p. 94.

14. *Virginia County Records: Albemarle County*, Book 11, p. 99, Andrew Hart Will (1832); Book 11, p. 146, Andrew Hart Inventory
(1833).

15. See *Montague's Richmond Directory and Business Advertiser, for
1850-1851, by William Montague, No. 1, Copyright secured, Richmond;
First Annual Directory of the City of Richmond to which is added a Business
Directory for 1859*, compiled by Eugene Ferslew (Richmond: Geo. W.
West, 1859), for example.

16. *Property Tax Book, City of Richmond, 1860*, 3rd District, p. 43,
#25, F. B. Hart.

17. Frank D. Fuller and Thomas H. S. Curd (comp.), *The Curd
Family in America* (Rutland, Vermont: The Tuttle Publishing Company, Inc., 1938). This genealogy has been reprinted by Thomas H.
S. Curd, Jr., *Supplement to The Curd Family in America* (Roanoke, Virginia, 1981). I am grateful to Mr. Curd for his kind help and encouragement in my research on the Curd family.

18. *Portrait and Biographical Record of Buchanan and Clinton Counties,
Missouri* (Chicago: Chapman Bros., 1893), p. 284.

19. *Ibid.*

20. *History of Callaway County, Missouri* (St. Louis: National Historical Company, 1884), pp. 639-641.

21. See Anne Firor Scott, *The Southern Lady, From Pedestal to Politics, 1830-1930* (Chicago: University of Chicago Press, 1970) and John C. Ruoff, "Frivolity to Consumption: Or Southern Women in Antebellum Literature," *Civil War History* 18 (September 1972), 213-229.

22. Carroll Smith-Rosenberg, "The Female World of Love and Ritual: Relations between Women in Nineteenth-Century America," *Signs*, I, 1 (Autumn 1975), 1-29.

23. Jeffrey, *Frontier Women: The Trans-Mississippi West 1840-1880* (New York: Hill and Wang, 1979), pp. 36-37.

24. Douglas, *The Feminization of American Culture*, p. 307.

25. Arthur Martine, *Martine's Hand-Book of Etiquette* (New York: Dick & Fitzgerald, Publishers, 1865), pp. 113 and 126.

26. Anne M. Boylan, "Evangelical Womanhood in the Nineteenth Century: The Role of Women In Sunday Schools," *Feminist Studies* 4, 3 (October 1978), 62-80.

27. Douglas, *Feminization of American Culture*, pp. 116-117.

28. Epstein, *Politics of Domesticity*, p. 48. See also, Glenda Gates Riley, "The Subtle Subversion: Changes in the Traditionalist Image of the American Woman," *The Historian*, XXXII, 2 (February 1970), 210-227.

29. This is not the pattern, interestingly enough, in many farm women's diaries, where much of the content is a listing of seasonal, weekly, or even daily tasks such as making meals. As Marilyn Ferris Motz pointed out in "Marking Time: Daily Journals of Nineteenth Century Rural Americans," a paper delivered at the Seventh American Studies Association Convention, 1979, rural diarists tended to make little personal commentary, but concentrated on their "relationship to the community and the natural environment. . . . The diarist records not a personal search for meaning but acceptance of a set of values assumed to be held by the community as a whole."

30. John Modell and Tamara K. Hareven, "Urbanization and the Malleable Household: An Examination of Boarding and Lodging in American Families," *Journal of Marriage and the Family* (August 1973), 467-479.

The situation with Mrs. McKinney was somewhat unusual. The Curd brothers owned the house which Mrs. McKinney kept and in which various unmarried Curds and their employees lived.

31. Missouri was settled at first largely by southerners and

slaveholders, although 95% of the slaveholders owned five or fewer slaves. In 1830 there had been one slave to every four-and-a-half whites. Missouri's population grew dramatically, especially during the 1850s. The growth was largely due to the migrations of northerners and immigrants from Italy and, especially, Germany. In 1860 there was one slave to every nine white inhabitants in Missouri. See William W. Parrish, *A History of Missouri, 1860-1875* Vol. III, (Columbia: University of Missouri Press, 1973), p. 7.

32. In Callaway County, January 1 was the day on which slaves were bought or hired.

"An interesting sidelight on slavery in Callaway is given in the *Missouri Telegraph* of January 4, 1861, which says: 'A large crowd of persons were in town on New Year's Day. A number of slaves were sold and hired, at reduced prices compared with the past years. Field hands that hired for over $200 last year were hired this year at $150. Women that were hired last year at $80 were hired on Tuesday at $55 and $65.' The custom at the time was for a master having more slaves than he needed to hire them by the year to other persons. The 'reduced prices' undoubtedly resulted from the agitation concerning slavery that was current at the time."

Ovid Bell, *Political Conditions in Callaway Before the Civil War Began*, privately published by the author, 1952, p. 8.

33. From *History of Callaway County, Missouri*, pp. 286-287.

34. Tristine Rainer, *The New Diary*, preface by Anaïs Nin (Los Angeles: J. P. Tarcher, Inc., 1978), p. 9.

35. Degler, *At Odds: Women and the Family in America from the Revolution to the Present* (New York: Oxford, 1980), p. 181.

36. Douglas, *Feminization of American Culture*, pp. 249-253.

37. A copy of Betsy Dew's newspaper obituary was sewed together and pasted inside the back cover of Sam's diary, along with other inspirational clippings from Presbyterian newspapers. The obituary is interesting because of its views on death as well as the way it defines the ideal evangelical woman:

OBITUARY
Died, July 27th, at Sunny Bank Albemarle, the residence of her father, W. D. Hart, Esq., Mrs. Thos. R. Dew, after a lingering illness of nearly two years.

In the departure of this young wife and mother we have another illustration of the truth, that "god moves in a mysterious way." An affectionate father and mother are bereaved of their last surviving child a mother is taken from two helpless children, a husband is bereft of a devoted wife and the church of Christ has lost one of her most precious members, one whose life bid fair to be of great future usefulness. But God in his mercy has given much to support under this heavy affliction. For months the deceased has had her eye fixed upon those mansions which Jesus went to prepare for his people and during all that time, no cloud intervened to obscure her celestial view. Christians who went to her bedside, went not to comfort, but to learn how a guilty sinner may "rejoice always" through "Christ that strengtheneth." There was nothing pharisaic in her righteousness, she did not thank God she was better than others, her song of thanksgiving was thanks be unto God for his unspeakable gift, the Saviour of sinners. The earth could have covered from our view, none of more native loveliness of character: Death could have taken none from our midst, amidst more universal weepings, but thanks be to God death shall lose its victory and the grave give up earth's loved ones in the morning of the resurrection. Death has no more dominion over her. Sickness, suffering and tears have all passed away for her, for in the presence of the Lord there is fullness of joy and at his right hand pleasures forevermore.

The Whig and Philadelphia Presbyterian will please copy.

38. David E. Stannard, *The Puritan Way of Death: A Study in Religion, Culture, and Social Change* (Oxford: Oxford University Press, 1977).

39. To give only a few prominent examples, see: Blanche Wiesen Cook (ed.), *Crystal Eastman On Women and Revolution* (Oxford: Oxford University Press, 1978); Sherna Gluck (ed.), *From Parlor to Prison: Five American Suffragists Talk About Their Lives* (New York: Vintage Books, 1976); Ann Sutherland Harris and Linda Nochlin, *Women Artists, 1550-1950* (New York: Alfred A. Knopf, 1979); David M. Kennedy, *Birth Control in America: The Career of Margaret Sanger* (New Haven: Yale University Press, 1970); Gerda Lerner, *The Grimke Sisters from South Carolina: Pioneers for Women's Rights and Abolition* (New York: Schocken Books, 1971); Kathryn Kish Sklar,

Catharine Beecher: A Study in American Domesticity (New York: W. W. Norton & Company, Inc., 1973).

40. For example, William H. Chafe, *Women and Equality: Changing Patterns in American Culture* (Oxford: Oxford University Press, 1977); Betty Friedan, *The Feminine Mystique* (New York: Dell Publishing Co., Inc., 1963); John S. Haller and Robin M. Haller, *The Physician and Sexuality in Victorian America* (New York: W. W. Norton & Co., Inc., 1974); Elizabeth Janeway, *Man's World, Woman's Place: A Study in Social Mythology* (New York: Delta Book, 1971); Sheila Rowbotham, *Woman's Consciousness, Man's World* (Harmondsworth Middlesex, England: Penguin Books, Inc., 1973); Ronald G. Walters (ed.), *Primers for Prudery: Sexual Advice to Victorian America* (Englewood Cliffs, N. J.: Prentice-Hall, Inc., 1974); and Kathryn Weibel, *Mirror, Mirror: Images of Women Reflected in Popular Culture* (Garden City, N. Y.: Anchor Books, 1977).

41. See, for instance, Nancy F. Cott, *The Bonds of Womanhood*; Barbara Leslie Epstein, *The Politics of Domesticity*; Mary Hiatt, *The Way Women Write* (New York: Columbia University, Teachers College Press, 1977); Amanda Porterfield, *Feminine Spirituality in America, From Sarah Edwards to Martha Graham* (Philadelphia: Temple University Press, 1980); Carroll Smith-Rosenberg, "The Female World of Love and Ritual"; Joelynn Snyder-Ott, "The Female Experience and Artistic Creativity," *Art Education*, Vol. 27, 6 (September 1974), 15-18; Patricia Meyer Spacks, *The Female Imagination* (New York: Alfred A. Knopf,) 1975); and Julia Penelope Stanley and Susan J. Wolfe (Robbins), "Toward A Feminist Aesthetic," *Chrysalis: A Magazine of Women's Culture*, No. 6, 57-71.

42. Johnny Faragher and Christine Stansell, "Women and Their Families on the Overland Trail to California and Oregon, 1842-1867," *Women's Experience in America: An Historical Anthology*, ed. Esther Katz and Anita Rapone (New Brunswick, N. J.: Transaction Books, 1980), p. 295, believe that most pioneer women resisted this heroism.

"The vicissitudes of the trail opened new possibilities for expanded work roles for women, and in the cooperative work of the family there existed a basis for a vigorous struggle for female-male equality. But most women did not see the experience in this way. They viewed it as a male enterprise from

its very inception. Women experienced the breakdown of the
sexual division of labor as a dissolution of their own auton-
omous "sphere." Bereft of the footing which this indepen-
dent base gave them, they lacked a cultural rationale for the
work they did, and remained estranged from the possibilities
of the enlarged scope and power of family life on the trail.
Instead, women fought against the forces of necessity to
hold together the few fragments of female subculture left to
them."

As noted above, Faragher in a later work revised his view that
women might achieve equality through work, but not his view
that women resisted the changes in work roles.

43. For instance, in a brochure advertising a 1979 humanities
institute sponsored by the Modern Language Association and the
National Endowment for the Humanities titled "Women's Words/
Women's Literature," Elizabeth Meese wrote that she looked for
excellence in women's writing in rather traditional terms:

"Revising the literary canon, to me, means the enfranchise-
ment of writers whose works were unfairly excluded. It
means the establishment of revised criteria for inclusion
rather than the abandonment of all standards. I still expect
writers to have an original perspective on human events. I
expect at least an implicit critique of culture. . . . I do not
wish to suspend the requisite need for language to emerge
from the writer's fundamental authenticity—something
again which requires an honesty about one's self and one's
world. Expression must be fresh, spontaneous, unselfcon-
scious."

44. See Ellen DuBois, Mari Jo Buhle, Temma Kaplan, Gerda
Lerner, and Carroll Smith-Rosenberg, "Politics and Culture
In Women's History: A Symposium," *Feminist Studies*, 6, 1 (Spring
1980), 26-64.
45. Sheila Rowbotham, *Woman's Consciousness, Man's World* (Harmondsworth, England: Penguin Books, 1973), p. xii.
46. Douglas, *The Feminization of American Culture*, pp. 10-11.
47. For instance, Ellen DuBois, in her part of "Politics and Culture in Women's History," p. 35, dismissed Wood's work in a foot-
note: "Wood, who was one of the earliest contributors to the con-

cept of women's culture, has since reversed her position and written a snide attack on ninetenth-century sentimentalists, *The Feminization of American Culture.*"

The Diary

M. Samuella Curd
Fulton, Mo.
August 8, 1860

M. S. Curd's Diary Commencing 3rd May 1860

May 3rd. On the evening of this day, the marriage ceremony of Mr. Thomas Curd, of Fulton, Missouri and myself was performed, by Rev. Charles H. Reid of Richmond Va. I had 8 brides-maids and grooms-men. viz, Missess Dandridge, Betty and Mag Hart, L & G Anderson, E George, Matt Curd, & M Brooks. Messrs Isaaic Curd, John Curd, W Tucker, G Durry & Anderson's. None but neighbors and attendants present. Directly after the ceremony we took supper, and left within an hour for Washington; there were nine in party, Fanny Gaines, & Mr. Seaton Linsley, of Hanover Va., who were married the night before, Miss Matt Curd, Betty Hart—Mr. John Curd. Mr. Wm. Tucker. Mr. Linsley Mr. Thomas Curd & myself made up the party. Traveled all night, arrived in Washington just at light,—stopped at Brown's Hotel.

May 4th. Part of the party spent the day sight seeing. I was not well enough to go out.

May 5th. Mr. Curd and myself went to Alexandria to see Aunt Julia Hart, while the others went sight seeing. Cousins Sarah & Henry came while we were gone, got back to late dinner & started off soon after for Baltimore amidst the shouts of the friends at the Hotel. Arrived in Baltimore just before dark. Went up to Mrs. Stevenson's after tea, had fun passing myself off to an old friend as Miss Hart.—Stopped at the Eutan.

May 6th. Spent the Sabbath in Balt-: Some went to Church. I staid with Matt Curd, who was sick, until after service, when Mr. Stevenson came for me & took me to his house to dine, spent the evening talking over old times with Anna! Mr. C. came for me about 5. o'clock. Did not go to Church that night—Mr. Dunning called to see us at the Eutan House.

May 7th. Started to Philadelphia, got there about 1 o'clock, stopped at the Continental, a new & splendid Hotel, elegantly fitted up, all were charmed, & concluded we had better spend the season there. Went out that evening to the Fair Mount Water Works, which are truly beautiful, & from the grounds the view of the City is very fine. A storm came on which hurried us back to the Hotel. The evening spent partly in my room, partly in the parlor a merry party & perfectly independant.

May 8th. Went to Laural Hill Cemetery. This is a lovely spot, some very handsome Tomb Stones, have a fine view of the Schuylkill from several points, went to Gerard College rode around town & returned to the Hotel to dinner. Mr. Scott, one of Dr. Curd's friends called to see us. Left for New York that evening, & arrived there by 9 O'clock that night, stopped at the St. Nicholas.

9th. The morning rainy and dreary looking. Cousin Eliza Price called to see us very early, sat some time, after she left Brother John, Matt, Betty and myself, went to ride, went up 5th. Avenue to 5th. avenue House. Looked over that, and from there went to Barnums Museum, met Mr. Curd there, staid some time and walked back to the Hotel. Brother J. and Matt went to cousin E's soon after dinner, the latter to spend the night. Mr. Linsley & Fanny, Betsy Hart & Dr. Linsley, Mr. Curd and myself went to the opera, Moses in Egypt. Dr. L. was gentlemanly and merry, but not too much to go with Betsy, was decidedly funny in the omnibus. The Academy of music, which is a splendid House, was filled. The opera was not very good, it was said. It was my first and I couldn't judge, it closed about 11. Walked back to the Hotel. Betty Dr. L., & myself took supper at 12 o'clock. The Dr. feeling very badly on account of his conduct—was extremely polite, Betsy treated him [torn.]

May 10th. Mr. Curd and Linsley took Fanny, Betsy and myself up to cousin Eliza's to get cousin C. Matt & Miss Temple, to go to the *"Womans rights Convention,"* dismissed the gentleman after getting there, & off we started to the Convention. It was raining, but the Hall was very well filled, I was shocked to see negro men and women take seats in the white congregation but nothing is too disgusting for them; The proceedings were contemptable, Cousin E was afraid Fanny & myself would be called to account for our conduct. Left quite soon, from there went to the Milliners. Matt, Fanny & myself each got an immense bonnet, mine & F's alike, Matt's purple; they were the tip of the fashion. Returned to cousin E's where the gentlemen joined us, and took us to the Academy of Design, where we were highly entertained for some time, from there went to the Hotel. I was too much fatigued to go to dinner. Matt and I had dinner sent to our rooms charged $2.00 extra, we had a *"heap"* of fun. Dr. L. came almost in the room whilst Matt was undressed, grand scampering. That evening all except Fanny, Seaton & the Dr. went to cousin E's by invitation, such a broken down set, was never seen. I felt as if I would drop, but had to keep up & talk as if nothing was the matter. Staid until 12 o'clock. the omnibus had stopped running had great trouble to get a hack. We could go no further. Fanny and Seaton staid at home to rest.

11th. Morning unlikely. All went to the Navy yard, but Matt & myself. I had too bad a cough to go out early. Mr. Curd came back sooner than the rest. It cleared off beautifully in the evening. Matt, Mr. Curd & myself, went to Green Wood Cemetery. Went over in the omnibus & horse car, got a hack after getting there & rode over the grounds. it is truly an enchanting spot, Nature & Art have contributed largely to its beauty. Many of the Tomb stones are splendid & the view of the bay from many points is very fine. Got back to the Hotel to *late* dinner the others of the party had returned, dressed for dinner & was just finishing when we made our appearance in the dining room, ate in our bonnets and traveling dress. We gave mutual accounts of the days proceedings. Betsy Hart was in trouble, had her pocket picked of $20.00 while on the omnibuss. That night cousin Eliza & Mr. Price came to see us. All went in & took supper together. After which cousin E said good bye & left & we retired, well broken down.

May 12th. Went out shopping directly, after breakfast, hurried back to start to Albany by half past nine O'clock, parted with brother John at the depot; and off we hurried to Albany, where we arrived at 5 o'clock, stopped at the Delevan House. Betsy Fanny Seaton & myself took a walk after dinner to see the City. Mr. Curd not very well & Matt not inclined to go. Had a pleasant stroll. Came to the Hotel in time for supper.

13th. Fanny & I went to church with Mr. Tucker and Lindsley, the others not disposed to go. Mr. C not well. At night *all* went to the Baptist Church heard a rare kind of sermon, which was somewhat amusing, cloudy & threatening rain when we returned.

14th. Started early this morning to Niagara had a long tiresome day's journey, got there in the night stopped at the International, took supper & retired as soon as possible.

15th. Morning bright and pleasant, started directly after breakfast to view this grand work of Nature, would that I had a pen of a ready writer, that I might do some *faint* justice to it; but to appreciate one *must see.* Were gone for some time, stopped at the Fancy Stores of Indian work, making some purchases. Matt, Mr. C. & myself went to the Hotel, the others went up in the *car* to get a better view of the Falls. After dinner took a ride over the Inspension bridge, and on the Canadian side all except Mr. Curd, Tucker, & myself dressed in oil cloth suits, the most horrid & dirty things I ever saw, and went down under the Falls, my cough was too bad to go. the girls and young men were the greatest sights imaginable, particularly Betsy Hart went to see the burning Spring. The old woman who showed excited for fear we would not pay her, as part of the party left before the others. From this to an old dilapidated wooden frame they called a "tower" from which we were promised to see wonders. I couldn't go but a short distance all pronounced it a *humbug*, this is the greatest place to fleece one of his money. Returned to the Hotel about dark, after taking a little rest went to supper, after this all met in my room; a noisy time we had, recounting the pleasures we had, since being together, & making mutual promises of writing to & remembering each other. It was an evening to me of peculiar sadness. We had been together for some days, & this was the eve previous to our sounding the sad word fare-well to those who were dear to me & who had lived with me under the same roof, my dear little sister, for she was much younger than I was. From this time the Scenes & whole Tenor of my life, would change. I would soon turn my face Westward away from the scenes of *home* and childhood, a new sphere of action would open before me, and on me in great measure must depend the making of a *home* happy or miserable, whilst talking & laughing these thoughts would crowd out others, and naturally made me sad. And as the last sound of good night fell on my ears, I could but ask, will we? can we ever meet thus again? and a voice within whispered, *never!*—

May 16th.   Rose early this morning to be ready to start, part of us westward, the other north-ward. Col. Quarles and Miss McAfee sent up their cards very early. Saw them a few minutes. All went down to breakfast, from thence to our rooms to put on bonnets & traveling gear, soon the cry omnibus ready, sounded & we were to go a short distance together. I felt too *deeply*, to talk, in a few minutes the final *good bye* must be said; and said it was in deep silence. Mr. Tucker, Matt Curd, Mr. Curd and myself taking the cars westward, & the others going across the lake up the St. Lawrence to Montreal. We traveled all day and arrived at Detroit that evening. Changed cars here, and started directly for Cincinnatti traveled all night.

17th.   Arrived in Cincinnatti at 9 o'clock this morning, the warmest day we have since leaving Richmond, put on the first summer dress for dinner. did not go out while in Cincinatti, stopped at the Burorch House.

18th.   Started at 1/2 past 4 o'clock for St. Louis traveled all day & until nine o'clock, went to Barnums. All very much fatigued.

19th.   Started early this morning for St. Aubert, the station at which we got off to go to Fulton. Arrived there about 1, o'clock the weather very warm. found only one hack with ten or twelve persons who wanted to go. Mr. Curd persuaded the driver to let us go first & then come for the others, this was done and Matt, Mr. Tucker, Mr. Curd & myself started for Fulton. It was thus I began to feel truly where I was, & how far I had left home friends away. but I resorted to my usual plan, laughed and talked, to conceal my feelings if nothing more. The roads were right good & went in hot haste. Arrived in Fulton early in the evening. Circumstances with me had greatly changed since I, two years previous to this, had entered the town, to pay as I thought my first & last visit.—Truly we know not "what a day may bring forth." The hack drove to Mrs. McKinney, which was to be my future home for a time. She met me with great kindness, & soon after cousin Mary Abbot, the Dr. & brother Ed came up to welcome us. I felt pretty badly. but think I concealed it. That night went to see aunt Ann who was a perfect cripple.

20th.   Sunday, was too fatigued to go to church, walked

around in the evening to see cousin Martha Dyer, who had been afflicted by the death of her son Edward. From this time till the 6th. of August I will not be able to give detailed account, but relate just as it comes to my mind. For some time, my time was taken up receiving and paying calls, we had a very *hot* spell of weather the week after I got to Fulton, heard from home and Va. friends quite often. After being cool for a short time we had another warm spell. The exercises of the Seminary & College commencement the 15th. of June and continued until the 28th. the weather was quite seasonable. 29th.   Fulton looked very genial—nearly all left this day. 30th.   Mr. Jimmy Quarles preached morning & night, most excellent sermons both of them. I fear his health will not be sufficient for his labors. Miss Kitty Diggs from Glascow, came down with him spent several days; they left on Monday. During commencement exercises there were some very good speeches, some of the young men acquitted themselves well. Said to be the best class since the College opened. Dr. Plummer spoke one night, most all were disappointed I don't think he did himself justice. There were two Cantations, one just before & the other during the Seminary commencement. Miss Mag Scott was queen in one the play being Queen Esther & Miss Tate as May queen in the other, both passed off very pleasantly. Every body that could, left after the schools closed. We have been without a preacher most of the time the Elders leading prayer meeting at the appointed times. Oh! that we could have one just Invited to our situation, sent to us, who would be a true sheperd to this wandering flock. The whole month of July has been excessively hot & dry for four weeks & more not enough rain fall to wet the ground an inch, vegetation parched & the cry for eatibles & water, with the worst cry of starvation has been sounded. But God reigneth & will not forsake us all together in withholding the latter rain. Since the 1st of August there has been very general rain in the country & some in town the crops though very much injured as they will not yield half as much as expected, are improved by the rain lately. I have never felt such a long spell of hot weather; it unfits one for almost every duty.

August 6th.   Weather excessively hot. To-day the elections of County & State officers comes off there with much excitement here. The polls did not close until 12 o'clock. & then a number did not vote. brother Ed elected as County Treasurer. I commenced to-day to keep a diary, going back in memory to the 3rd of May & writing up.

7th. The town quite full of people who staid after the Elections. Went to church at night. Mr. Mechat lead prayer meeting. Great excitement in town, display of burning tar barrels, sky rockets & every variety of sound the human voice could make. A number of speeches made returns came that St. Louis is to have a black Republican candidate or representative in Congress.

8th. Morning very warm, had a fine shower in the evening, which made it delightful. Mr. Curd brought up a bucket of the littlest green peaches I most ever saw. Mrs. McKinney went down at night to see Mrs. Karns. I have the blues to be at home.

9th. Today has been delightful, cousin Mary came up to spend the morning. Matt went to see Mrs. Wells & Manchester. Henry Watkins here in the evening. Mrs. McKinney and Matt spent the night with cousin Sue, her baby very ill. Went to church at night & heard an excellent sermon from Mr. James Baird. Came home & ate a watermelon.

10th. Mrs. Wells & Bick Dyer spent the day at Mrs. McKinneys, both so pleasant.—Mrs. Fisher called in the evening, Matt & myself went to see cousin Lizzie Dyer in the evening. Mr. Baird preached at night, I was not well enough to go Mr. Curd staid with me, Matt & Mrs. McKinney staid the night with cousin Sue Tuttle. Heard from Richmond.

11th. Spent the morning with cousin Sue, nursed her sick baby, went to cousin Mary Abbot's in the evening & to church at night with the baby. The Union party had a torch light procession in honor of Rollins election. very poor affair.

Aug 12th. Went to church morning & night, heard Mr. Baird. Like the morning sermon, was greatly fatigued before he finished the night sermon. Had a nice musk-melon in the evening, cousin Mary Abbot came by from cousin Sue's & called in to get some.

13th. Was quite unwell all morning—slept several hours. Mrs. McKinney staid up to cousin Sue's until dinner, went there directly after dinner & staid until I went up at four o'clock, the baby grew worse until 2 o'clock when it exchanged the pains of this life, for one of Eternal bliss. Cousin Mary & Dr. Abbot & family spent the evening staid until 10 o'clock Mr. Curd went to the P.O., brought me a letter from Andy Calhoun, announcing the death of Betsy Dew. oh! how mysterious are the ways of Providence, we have here verified the fact Death loves a shining mark, truly a bright star has gone out in, from the circle of her acquaintances & relations. Many there will be to drop the tear of sympathy over her grave. Oh! that the living might improve by these repeated warnings.

14th.   Went to cousin Sue's early in the morning, from there to Mrs. Humphreys to see Lou Cordell's baby it is very sick, the funeral of cousin Sue's baby preached this evening. Mrs. Mc went to prayer meeting, my head ached too much to be there. Heard from home tonight.

15th.   The day passed quietly, helped Matt on her black silk dress. did my usual reading in the morning, went to cousin Sue's soon after dinner, & from there to see Lou Cordell's baby which is very ill. Matt went to Judge Hockaday's came back stewing no body at home that long walk for nothing. Matt & Mrs. Mc. sent for to go to Lou's directly after supper, the 6th. night they have been there. got a letter from Betsy tonight; John Anderson's baby dead! mighty hot in [unreadable line].

16th.   Weather changed to be warmer in the morning & *very* warm in the evening. Lou Cordell's child died at 12 o'clock, went there directly after dinner. Looked so natural. Lou had a great deal of fortitude. Went to aunt Martha's after tea.

August 17th.   Spent the morning with cousin Mary Abbot, quite warm when I came back, finished my pillow cases; marked them after dinner & went to see Bick Dyer, & from there to Mrs. Lawther.

18th.   Felt very badly all the morning. Mrs. Mc & Matt went to church I laid down while they were gone, felt better in the evening cousin May & Betty Nicholson were here spent a pleasant evening. Matt & Mrs. Mc went to church at night, quarterly meeting in the Methodist Church.

19th.   Betty Nicholson here staid last night. I went to church twice heard an Irish Preacher Mr. Morton, from Mal: 3rd 19th. in the morning & in the evening from 2nd Tim: 2nd 19th. Mr. Monroe the Methodist Preacher dined here today.

20th.   After my usual reading, went to cousin Sue's, staid until dinner time, had a pleasant shower, which cooled the air, but not enough to do vegetation any good, rained some in the evening. Looked for brother John, but did not come I felt impatient to see all at home. Poor me so far from all.

21st. Dreadfully home sick. Can I *ever* get weaned from home? Mrs. Karns here this morning. Did but little to day felt so indolent. Went to church at night heard most excellent remarks from Mr. Mechat, he became quite overcome in his prayers. Oh! that the whole church might be more deeply moved at our sad condition. God grant a union of spirit. Expected to hear from home, but was disappointed.

22nd. Spent the morning with cousin Mary Abbot & staid to dinner the first time I have eaten from Mr. Curd. Came home & peeled peaches for putting up. went to bed very soon.

23rd. Staid at home, helped Matt make cake for a party. All discouraged at the complete failure in baking. Various conjectures as to the cause. Matt & Mrs. Mc went to Mr. Hawkins funeral. I staid at home and laid down. Went to Mrs. Knolly's to the first meeting of the female prayer meeting, only 3 there besides those at home, had a pleasant meeting. Mrs. Mc. & Matt went to prayer meeting, Mr. Curd & I staid at home.

August 24th. Tried some more cake, a total failure again. Matt very discouraged, sent some to cousin Mary's to bake, but no better than ours. In the evening Whiling and Thom Diggs came from Glascow. Mrs. Mc. went to Mrs. Karns. Matt has neuralgy again disappointed in not seeing Brother John. No rain distressingly dry every thing burnt up.

25th. Henry Watkins spent the day here, had a very pleasant time. After dinner, I went to the Asylum & Institute, from there to Mr. Vandoren & took tea at cousin Sam Dyers, got home found all gone. Brother John came in the St. Aubert stage, did not come up that night.

26th. Brother J came up to breakfast looks well didn't let Matt know he had come until he got here. Went to church heard Mr. Morton can't say I was much benefitted. Sermon long & I had a headache. Which lasted all morning so I couldn't go to Church, Bro. J., Mr. C. myself staid at home.

27th. Staid at home all day nothing of interest happened.

28th. Mr. Curd sick last night. At home all morning Mrs. McKinney a sick headache, in great trouble about her sons.

29th. Busy all day fusing for a party. Matt had dreadful luck with her cake. There were a number present. All seemed to enjoy themselves, the weather was very warm, got a letter from home, sorry to hear of Mr. Robinson's failure.

52 SAM CURD'S DIARY

30th. Went to Mr. Robert Dyer's in the wagon, to spend the day, had a pleasant time, very comfortably fixed had a light shower in the evening, but there is still great want of water for man and cattle, a want entirely new to me.

31st. Went to Mr. Snells in the wagon to spend the day, came back at 4, when Brother John went to Mr. Nicholson's. I had a sick headache.

September 1st. Matt & Mrs. Mc. went to the country to a big Methodist meeting. I am alone, but not lonesome, made some peach preserves. In the evening Henry & Matt & Watkins & the Diggs came around. Henry staid to supper, a pleasant evening. Cousin Mary Abbott came after tea & of course there was an agreeable time.

September 2nd. The day passed in the normal order of things. Several came in to see me.

3rd. No preaching or meeting of any kind. The first Sabbath such a thing has happened since I came to Fulton. The cause of religion is truly in a sad condition at this time. God grant a better time quickly. Went to the Elders prayer meeting in the evening at Mayor Knolly's. The question there discussed as to the best plan to endeavor to have a better state of things in the Pres: church. No decided plan was taken, *they* not agreeing.

4th. Spent the morning at aunt Martha's. Whiling Diggs came home with Matt to dinner. Miss Karnes & Mrs. Robinson here in the evening. Went to Dr. Abbott's to tea, to meet *Hon.* Mr. Birch & Lady from California.

5th. Had someone with me all day. Went to a children's party at aunt Martha's in the evening. all seemed to enjoy themselves got a long letter, was sister, she is better satisfied. *Very, very* warm.

6th. Jimmy Nicholson here a little while. Went to cousin Sue's. Female prayer at Major Nolly's not but two present. hope it may increase in numbers & be the instrument of much good. Had a bad head-ache.

7th. Matt & Mrs. McKinney came home, had a nice time, & first rate preaching wish we had some here. Mrs. Karns went to house-keeping to-day. All from aunt Martha's here at night. Henry going off to teach, felt so sorry to say good bye to her.

8th. Have a bad headache this morning laid down until 10 o'clock. Matt went to church. Mrs. Mc. to see Mrs. Karns. Cousin Mary came up in the evening felt in very good spirits until late in the evening. feel *now* (this is about six o'clock, every thing out doors, looking as dreary & gloomy as possible) about as gloomy as the weather. Oh! what would I not give to see my dear home. Just one sight would do me good. There has been a violent change, from hot to cool fall weather. This is life we know not what a day may bring forth.

September 9th.   Went with cousin Sue out to White Cloud, heard Mr. Morton preach to a larger Congregation. He united with the church. Oh! that *we* might see such a scene in *our* church. Came back to dinner & went to hear Mr. Mayhew preach for the last time here.

10th.   Every thing went on as usual, aunt Ann came in the evening, went down to see her. Henry had a baby to-night, born dead. Mrs. Mc & Matt went to spend the night with Mrs. Karns.

11th.   All things occurred in the usual routine.

12th.   Matt went to Conference this morning, Mrs. Mc. to Mrs. Karns & I to cousin Sue. In the evening I went to prayer meeting no-body there, am afraid we will not be able to establish one.

13th.   Nothing new under the sun happened with us today.

14th.   Felt very unwell all day. cousin Mary here in the evening. Miss Bristo staid all night with Mrs. Mc.

15th.   Every prospect of a good rain, but not enough fell to settle the dust. Oh! for a good rain, the future can alone reveal, what will become of us unless we have rain. Went to aunt M's after tea.

16th.   Went to Methodist Church in the morning & heard the most indifferent sermon told Mr. C. that was what I gained by leaving my church, heard Mr. Horton at night—liked him.

20th.   Started with Charlie Abbott in a buggy to Boonville, at half past 5 o'clock went on finely for 10 miles when we found the back spring of the buggy was broken. Stopped 3/4 an hour to have it fixed started off in constant fear we would have a tumble, went well 2 1/2 miles when we had to stop 1 1/2 hours, to have it mended. After this we went with a dash the roads were in splendid order. Got to Mrs. Bell's at half past 4 O'clock, all astonished to see me & thought we made a most rapid trip, found all in high fire to go to Texas, intend to go by land, quite an adventure, cousin seems very feeble, lies down most of the day, thinks the trip will benefit her, felt less fatigued then I expected.

September 21st.   Went as soon as breakfast was over to Boon-

ville, my first visit was to Mrs. Bowers, surprised to see me. I asked
if she knew me. Yes, the same old Sam Hart. Mrs. Bell went for
Mr. Lionberger, without telling him who was there. He was too
astonished to know me, all said he was to confused forgot to take a
kiss. Then went to see Mr. Johnson, it was pleasant to meet old
friends & see they had not forgotten me. Mr. Lionberger's family in
affliction heard today of Judge Richardson's death; he will be
greatly missed in St. Louis. Went back to Mrs. Bell's in the heaviest
dust. The clouds seem as if they would never again give rain.

22nd.   Staid at cousin L's all day, felt *very* badly from the ride, as
the excitement wore off. Cousin L & Eliza went to town in the
evening. I took a short ride on horse-back, which made me feel
worse.

23rd.   Went to Boonville to church, it was most suffocating
with dust, saw few at church. Most of these were strangers,
Boonville so much changed. Came home almost broken down.
Went to bed directly after dinner & did not get up until night. Mr.
B. staid away all night.

24th.   Too unwell to get up this morning. Soon after breakfast
was cheered with a visit from Bell Lionberger, now Mrs. Woolfolk,
she looks beautiful. Was so glad to see her & she seemed the same.
In bed all day the first day since I was married.

25th.   Lizzie Allen came this evening. She is well & very fleshy,
talks about Mr. Cope as if he were something great. *What taste.*
begged me to come & see her.

26th.   The day passed quietly. No one came.

27th.   Mr. & Mrs. Hoge came this morning, Miss H. looks just
as she did 3 years ago. She spent the day & we returned with her; it
must be very lonely for her out there no near neighbors, every
thing so different from what she has been used to. Got a package
of letters one from Mr. Curd, one from father. all well.

September 28th.   Andy, Eliza & myself out to Mr. Hoge's, spent a
pleasant day cutting up all sorts of capers. Andy in a great glee.

29th.   All went in the wagon to spend the day at Col. Quarles.
He seems to have tried to bury his house. All the arrangements,
like a confirmed bachelor. Had an excellent dinner. He is out of
sorts about Mrs. Barr's marriage. Cousin L & Gilmer came to Mr.
Hoge's in the evening.

30th.   Morning gloomy, clouds threatening had a very good
rain, but not near enough for the wants of the people. Went to

church, very few there on account of the weather. Mr. Bell gave a good practical sermon. My eyes hurt so badly in the evening, could not read, so slept most of the evening. Sang a long time after supper.

October 1st.   Went to Mrs. Russel's with cousin Lavenia. She is in great trouble just heard of son's death of whom she did not know he was sick, so uneasy about cousin Angy. Want Eliza to go to Texas but is afraid she might be sick & she could not see her. Staid there to dinner, came to Mrs. B's in the evening.

2nd.   Went to Boonville, first to Mrs. Bower's then to see Lizzie Allen. She was out on the fair grounds. Visited Mrs. Hood & Smith the latter looks wretchedly. Went to Mrs. Bowers to dinner, in the afternoon walked around town. Town greatly changed, & while the appearance as far as building is concerned has improved. Yet from outward signs there must be great dissipation. The State of Religion seems low here. Oh! that our churchs might be revived if there were more religion there would be less disputation. The church needs purifying.

3rd.   Went to the Fair grounds, was with Bell all day. She has not changed much but yet 3 years will make some changes. Saw a number of old friends, did not seem to be forgotten.

October 4th. Went from Bell's to the Fair grounds, spent a delightful day, seeing my friends, had a long talk over old times with Bell.

5th.   Had a good rain early this morning, but went to the Fairgrounds. The day passed as usual, quite an accident happened in the evening there was something of a Tournament & in riding around the point of one of the Spears was dashed off by accident but flew into a man's face & injured him severely Went to Mr. Bells in the evening.

6th.   Went to Mr. Hoge's in the evening with Gilmore & Mr. Bell, spent the night there.

7th.   Went to church, very attentive congregation, & a solemn sermon. Collection taken up for the new church, got nearly $200. Mr. & Mrs. Nichol dined with Mrs. Hoge Gilmer & Mr. Bell. Went home in the evening, how I hated to tell them good bye, maybe forever.

8th.   Started to Columbia this morning, the roads were horrible. Looked the jumping off point to creation. Got to Mr. Lymans about night, spent a most pleasant night.

October 9th.   Mr. Lyman went with us to Columbia. Mr. H & myself went to the City Hotel, staid there during Synod, it is an excellent House, roomed with a Mrs. Sermin from Glascow, who came down with Mr. Jimmy Quarles. Liked her so very much. Mr. Hoge staid at Mr. Todds.

10th.   Presbytery met this morning, preaching tonight by Mr. Paxton from Arrow Rock, slim congregation, everybody went to hear Bishop Hawks. The church records were the order of the day, discussion as to the relative relation of deacons & elders trouble in Mr. Marchmore's church. Oh! for a deeper toned piety, & that these troubles would be healed. God grant this meeting may be blessed to this town.

11th   Synod opened with a sermon from President Laws, finely prepared discourses, but not suited for spiritual food, or growth. Mr. Cochran chosen Moderator. Saw a number of Fulton people, was so glad to meet them, am anxious to get home.

October 11th   Went to Synod this morning, preaching at 11 o'clock, very few in attendance, Synod met downstairs. Went to Mrs. Pierce to dine, she is very nicely fixed, met several preachers there. Went to the church in the evening & from there to the Hotel.

12th   No preaching today. Judicial case of Mr. Abbott's of St. Louis on hand; moved & 2nd that the session be held with closed doors, so off we left. Went to Mrs. Ferguson's & from there to the Hotel with Mr. VanDoren, he called for me at half past 12 o'clock & went with me to Mr. Stephens to dine, took tea at Mrs. Fergerson's.

13th   Synod with open doors today, busy with the Abbott case he was allowed 3 1/2 hours to defend himself & the Prosecutor Dr. Coynes from St. Louis the same time, tiresome discussion. Preaching at night, took tea at Mr. Robert Todd's. The Fulton case came up tonight.[1] Mr. Tate made a speech stating in plain terms the whole trouble of the church. Mr. Laws replied synod adjourned before he finished. Went this evening to the University grounds, the situation is fine, the rooms of the society very nice, have a splendid collection of minerals & shells. Like the President Minor very much. Dined today with Mrs. Todd, people so hospitable.

14th   Mr. Brooks preached a most delightful sermon from the text, "It is well with the righteous." He is a charming speaker, but Providence ways are mysterious, his throat is so much affected he could scarcely get through the sermon. Communion Service in the evening. Dr. Myers preached a sermon Mr. Cochran & Gallaher officated at the service, Mr. C. referred to the time when Synod was in Columbia 27 years ago. What a glorious revival followed & asked why it would not be so now. All things were ready if Christians would only plead. Heard Mr. Lighters at night.

October 15th   Started to Fulton in the stage with Mrs. Barber & Mr. Purvines, all begged me to stay until Tuesday to hear the Fulton case was decided; but I was anxious to get back. found all quite well Mr. Curd had been quite sick, while I was away did not hear of it, so glad to be back again.

16th   Went to see aunt Ann this morning for a little while could not stay long, old Mrs. Robinson was here spending the day. Aunt A. is about as usual, her sight is failing her very fast. but such Christian resignation I never saw.

17th   Riped up my travelling dress, & commenced making it over. Misses Henderson & Baber, came to make a call.

18th   The day passed as usual.

19th   Spent the morning with cousin Mary Abbott and the evening with cousin Lizzie Dyer. Heard from home yesterday, father has given up business until Spring.

20th   Finished my travelling dress & fixed my bonnet.

21st   Went to Sunday school for the first time, very few scholars, very little interest seems to be taken in it. Had prayer meeting this morning. Prospects dark, for obtaining a minister. Oh! For a gracious revival here.

22nd   Staid in doors all day weather charming more like the Spring than Fall. Greatly in need of rain. Cut out my new calico dress. Matt had a violent headache.

23rd   Sewed all morning, went to Mrs. Carr's in the afternoon, with Fanny Barlow, & at night to prayer meeting. Mr. Carr led the meeting, he spoke very feelingly upon the subject of the troubles of the church & urged them to exercise christian forbearance & forgiveness.

24th   Spent the morning with cousin Mary, came home to dinner, found company from the country, cousin M. called in the evening, & we went to female prayer meeting at cousin Sue Tuttle's, had Mrs. Carr, VanDoren, Harrison, Barbour, Abbott, Miss Monroe & Patton & myself. It was a delightful meeting. I trust it may be greatly blessed. God grant us a spirit of prayer. Went to hear Father Henry at night, a most solemn appeal from the text, "Thou shall die and not live." Tena Watkins went up to be prayed for.

October 25th   Went to prayer meeting at the Methodist church; but few in attendance, but I trust it was for the good of those who were there. Mr. Hersy is truly the most godly man I ever saw. Preached last night a solemn sermon.

26th   Went to prayer meeting at the Methodist Church, still very few there. I enjoyed it very much & felt that it was good to be there. From there went to see Mrs. Grant; but she was not in. Came home, had a bad headache all evening could not go to Church at night. Weather warm as Spring sitting with doors & windows open, distressingly dry.

26th   Had a right good shower, but not enough to fill the water courses, or cisterns, still much need of water. This morning went to prayer meeting. It was truly good to be there. Oh! where the petitions went up for ungodly husbands, I felt as if I could cry aloud & plead for my dear husband. God grant his salvation speedily.[2] Went to aunt Martha's in the evening, found her unwell & low spirited, went to church at night, heard Dr. Calhoun preach from the text, "They that be whole need not a physician."

27th   Went to Sabbath School, found very few present. To preaching night & morning.

28th   Went to prayer meeting at the Methodist church, had a most delightful sermon, felt it good to be there.

29th   At prayer meeting at the Methodist church in the morning. In the evening went to see aunt Martha & took her to see aunt Ann, quite a rain came down. I hurried home, don't know how aunt Martha got home. No prayer meeting at the church, or I didn't go on account of the rain.

30th   Nothing unusual happened to-day.

31st   Cloudy & damp all day think there will be rain soon.

November 1st   Rained last night, this morning it is raining & showing the first winter day we have had. Looks as if there will be a sleet. The house is not finished I am afraid they can't work for some time, had they come up to the Contract it would have been done.[3]

2nd   Raining fast all day real winter. Sewed closely all day, fast day & prayer for the good of the Nation.

November 3rd   Cloudy in the morning, but cleared off by noon, windy & disagreeable, went out in the evening to hunt Sunday school schollars, had the promise of five. Very tired when I came back.

4th   Went to Sunday school, I found all the little girls but one, who was sick, hope I shall have an interesting class, when fully arranged. Mr. Montgomery preached in the morning and at night.

5th   Bright & beautiful. *Fall* weather at home in the morning. Mrs. Jimmie Robertson here in the afternoon. Went to cousin Mary's to spend the evening, a pleasant time. Heard from home tonight all well, think father's letter read as if he were depressed in spirits, hope it is not so.

6th   Every thing passed off as usual until dinner. Bled Karns sent for Mrs. McKinney saying she was sick. Mrs. Mc. went directly, soon after sent for aunt Phillis. All things seemed to be getting on well. Until dark Bled grew impatient & insisted on taking chloroform, about an hour after she was taken with spasms, at half past 8 o'clock the Dr. took away her baby, but there was no change of any matter. She had spasms until 10 o'clock, when her spirit took its flight to Heaven as all believe.[4] Poor Mrs. Mc She has sore troubles, but God seems gracious with his consolations to her. Mr. Karns is very rebellious.

November 7th   Funeral preached by Mr. Bouland on this evening at Presbyterian Church at 3 o'clock, house filled a most consolatory sermon, "Blessed are the dead who die in the Lord." God grant it may be blessed to *all*.

8th   Weather gloomy. Mrs. Mc. enjoying to a happy measure the consolations of religion. She is burning with love to all, a privilege to be in her chambers. Oh! that we all may profit by Bled's death. God grant my dear husband may be warned. Oh! the conversion of his soul, I desire of above all earthly things. God give me *believing faithful prayers!*

9th   I was taken sick in the night—was sick for several hours & sick all day the first day since I came to Missouri I have laid down all day. News has come that Lincoln is elected. Mr. & Mrs. Wilson, Major Knolly & Mrs. Ford here to night.

November 10th   Day passed as usual. Mrs. M went in the evening to assist Mr. Karns to move, Aunt Martha spent the evening with us, company most of the day.

11th   Went to Sunday school had a full class, number of schollars increased. Mr. Morton preached this morning.

12th   Staid at home all day. Nothing especial happened.

13th   Weather bright & Spring like, sitting out in the porch, went to see Mrs. Harrison in the evening. Mrs. Mc & Matt spend the night with aunt Martha. Brick work of the house finished.

14th   Spent the morning with cousin Mary. Mrs. McIntire's funeral, preached this evening, an afflicted family. Matt & Mrs. Mc. went to Mrs. Bloodwater's at night, Mrs. Jane & Barbour sat with Mr. Curd & myself until bed time. Weather delightful. Heard from Mr. Bell's family all well & much pleased with camp life.

15th   Mr. Diggs & Miss Kitty came in the evening. Miss K & myself went to the female prayer meeting larger number present than has ever been. Elder's prayer meeting here at night. The first Mite party at Mrs. Kerr's to night.⁵ I did not go as Bled had died so lately, pleasant time I hear they had.

16th   Mrs. Watkins, Betty Nicholson & Miss Lawther dined here, spent the evening with cousin Mary. disappointed in not hearing from home.

17th   Cousin Sue, spent the day here, Miss Kitty & Wm. Diggs &ᶜ went to Mr. Nicholson's, Oh! I am so home sick; what would I not give to see my dear home. I feel so wretched about it, had a cry to night, but tried to cheer up when Mr. Curd came home.

18th   Sunday school I went full class, prayer meeting afterwards.

19th   Spent the evening at cousin Sue with Miss K, Wm. Diggs, Mr. Abbot, Mrs. Walker & Betty Nicholson & all of us. hope to hear from home.

20th   Miss K and Mr. Diggs went home this morning. Miss them much, Mrs. M. & Matt went to Mrs. Walkins & spent the night. I went visiting with cousin Mary, went to prayer meeting Oh! how sad to see how this privilege is neglected. No word from home.

21st & 22nd   Nothing unusual happened. 22nd it was snowing fast.

23rd   Very cold, & wintry, ground covered with snow. No letter yet, oh!

24th   Very cold,

25th   Went to Sunday school as usual. have a nice little class.

25th & 26th   Moderated, slow misty rain, cousin M. here.

26th   evening the night of the mite society.

27th   Went to prayer meeting to-night, went to see cousin Virginia & aunt Ann to-day.

28th   Things went on as usual.

29th   Thanksgiving day, went to Mrs. Van Doren's to dine, exercises at College in the morning, at church at night Mr. Marchmore with us. God grant us a blessing in this meeting.

30th   Prayer meeting this morning, preaching to night.

31st   Cold and bright. Matt spent the day at Mr. Wilson's. Sad times of the nations each night—greater causes for alarm. God preserve us! Open society at the College. Had a state the right to iscede the question.

December 1st   Sermon this morning preparatory to communion, a most solemn & searching sermon, truly Mr. Marchmore, will clear his skirts of the blood of sinners in this place. May each Christian preach it over in their lives. Preaching at night.

2nd   Went to Sunday school, prayer meeting before preaching, a most excellent sermon from Mr. Marchmore, communion services were unusually solemn to me & I hope blessed to the growth of grace in my heart, but oh! the anguish it gives me to separate from Mr. Curd, in all things united but separated here. God grant this may be the last time.

3rd   Prayer meeting at 12, o'clock. Preaching at night to be kept up, all the week. Mr. Marchmore has truly seen his duty, & I hope it may be blessed.

5th   To unwell to go out to-day. Mr. Kemper asked the forgiveness of the church. Heard from home yesterday, father writes of cousin Adrian Louder, being killed in a shooting affair about Politicks. Oh! how hear-rending to his poor mother.

4th 5th 6th 7th 8th   Prayer meeting twice a day and preaching at night, I have been every time but one day, became broken down.

9th   Went to Sunday school, found all my schollars there, though it was rainy bad day. Mr. Marchmore preached to a full congregation, prayer meeting in the evening, preached at the College at night.

10th, 11th & 12th   The meeting still progressing, with much succes, especially among the Students. Mr. Marchmore deals faithfully with the people.

13th, 14th & 15th   The usual meetings, I have become so broken down as not able to attend but twice a day it is a great privation. Aunt Ann was quite sick Friday night, went there Saturday & spent the day, or rather dined. Met Col. Tate there. Mr. Laws came to see Mrs. McKinney & had a long talk, I hope all things will get straight.

16th   Sick last night, this morning not able to get up until just before church. Went to church at 11 o'clock, the house crowded, 20 united with the church, making 29 or 31, I don't know which, the sermon was most excellent, & the services very solemn. Too unwell to go out at night I staid at home & read to Mr. Curd.

17th & 18th   The same services going at church. Dr. Overton professed conversion. Oh! that such might be the case with my dear ungodly husband.

19th & 20th   Prayer meeting 20*th* at Dr. Howard's. Mrs. Kern came by & took me out in her carriage, not well enough to be out at night, one good sign Mr. C. went alone.

21st   Snowing fast, real wintry day.

22nd   Very cold, did not go out to night.

23rd   No Sunday school, Mr. Marchmore preached, 8 joined the church in the morning, 2 at night making in all 44. Meeting closed to night.

24th   Snowed fast. Matt & Mrs. McKinney busy making Xmas fixings. I went in the snow to see cousin Martha who is sick.

25th   Xmas, the children were up looking after their stockings,[6] went to Methodist Church in the morning, dined at cousin Sue's six or seven there went to prayer meeting at night & after church sleigh riding twas glorious. I feel as sad as possible fear that something is the matter.

26th   Dined at Dr. Abbott's. Ginny invited to a party at Mr. Law's.

27th   Mite Society met at Mrs. Barbour's.

28th   Raining & snowing all day.

29th   Took tea at Mrs Henderson's and then went to the Mite Party at Dr. Abbott's after supper, rooms crowded.

30th   Mr. Marchmore preached.

January 1st (1861).   Today is bright and mild over head bad walking. Went to cousin Virginia's, this morning the students are calling in *droves*, on the ladies. The children gave a party there to night. Prayer meeting night, Mrs. Allen left when Mr. Laws spoke, sad case.

2nd   Matt & myself spent several hours at Mrs. Barbour's very pleasantly. We with Mr. Curd went to see Henry Watkins after tea. *no news.*

3rd   Henry too sick to go this morning, Ginny & Betty Nicholson here, Ginny & myself searched the town for worsted patterns & crochet rings. Went to female prayer meeting no one, but Mrs. Kerr & myself, cold evening.

4th   General fast day over the United States, Mr. Marchmore preached a long but good sermon; female prayer meeting in the evening, service at night, fast on account of the state of the Country, observed generally, stores closed.

5th   Warm & bright, but bad walking, no better news in politicks, truly these are distressing times, our help only is in God.

6th   To Sunday school as usual, all the class there but one. Mr. Marchmore preached in the morning, went to the Methodist church at night. Mr. Bouland preached on the condition of the country, the great need of prayer.

7th   Spent the day at Dr. Abbott's, female prayer meeting in the evening this is a week of prayer for the conversion of the World, meeting every night at the College.

8th   Everything passed as usual, weather damp cool & gloomy.

9th   Staid at home worked busily on a pair of slippers for father. The country still distracted.

10th   Went to cousin Lizzie Dyer's & Mr. Van Doren's Eliz. Van Doren & Sam sick in bed. everybody suffering with cold.

11th   Mrs. McKinney went to the country. Matt & myself to see aunt A. Nothing new the whole country in great excitement, North Carolina & Mississippi have seceded. No hope of better things, truly Christians should be earnest in prayer.

12th   Day is bright & warm, walked downtown in the evening Ginny had 2 teeth pulled.

13th   To Sunday school & Church as usual. No services at night.

14th   News came tonight Alabama & Florida had seceded. Distressing times!!! Mite Society met at cousin Virginia's good many out, drissling & muddy. Matt joined a writing class to-day. Mr. Curd staid at home all day. Made an attempt to make Molasses Candy, after wasting our strength out—it turned to molasses.

15th   Raining all day. Matt went to take her writing lesson. Mr. Marchmore came home with her. Staid until church time, only 4 ladies at prayer meeting. No news in politicks.

16th   The day passed off as usual.

17th & 18th   The same old style.

19th Spent the day at Dr. Abbott's went to cousin Sue's in the evening. Mrs. Jane Barbour took tea here. Heard that Mrs. Ev Price had a baby married only 8 months 4 days. Sad.

20th Went to Sunday school, & church, Sunday school more flourishing. Mr. Marchmore has decided to stay here.

22nd Staid closely in doors. Matt went to writing lessons.

23rd Went to see aunt Ann & from there to Mr. Lawther's to dine. Mrs. Kerr, Henderson, Knolly, their respective gentlemen, Matt & myself had everything No. 1 style.

23rd Snowing & hailing all day. Mr. Bouland here in the evening his visits are truly beneficial such piety in all his conversion, I feel greatly condemned. Mrs. McKinney still away.

24th Went to female prayer meeting this evening only three there. Mrs. Kerr, Barbour & myself; but I enjoyed it & felt strengthened by going. There is a great disturbance in College.[7] A number have been suspended & others expelled for not informing on their fellow Students. I am afraid there will be trouble.

January 25th Mrs. McKinney came this evening. Mr. Dunn came tonight. I went to see Aunt Ann, Mrs. Mc to see Mr. Karns, he never come here.

26th Bright & mild, streets very muddy. Mr. Dunn here this evening & at night. I wonder, how matters stand between him & Matt. Letter from home & Betty Anderson. Hard times the universal cry it is indeed straitened times with business men, & not much hope of things growing better.

27th Went to church & Sunday school, the latter very flourishing, Went to hear Mr. Mayhue at night. Mrs. Mc had a sick headache. Cousin Sue had another mishap, poor woman.[8]

28th Mr. Curd getting ice. Went to cousin Sue's in the evening. She is better.

29th Went to see aunt Ann & little while in the morning, Mr. Mayhue dined here, commenced quilting my quilt this evening, went to prayer meeting at night.

30th At home all day. Matt & Mrs. Mc both out this evening. Mr. C. staid up here until after 4 o'clock. Mite Society at Mrs. Kerr's to night, went with Mr. Mayer & Mrs. Abbott. Mr. Curd's cold too bad to go, had a pleasant evening. Not many out, got back by 11 o'clock.

31st Went to prayer meeting this evening but three of us there, but I felt it was good to be there.

February 1st   Mr. Dunn came tonight, Matt pretended to be surprised at seeing him.

2nd   Cloudy & threatening all day, until just about night, cleared off brightly. Mr. Dunn spoke at the Court House. Matt, cousin A & myself went, Such a sight—the crowd presented quite as great variety as you often see at a manegrie.[9] Mr. D made a right good speech, followed by Karns & McIntyre. The atmosphere of the crowd so disagreeable we left.

3rd   Services as usual, did not go out at night, not well enough.

February 4th   Went with Miss Janet Humphrey's to four places visiting, went alone to Judge Henderson's in the afternoon. Mrs. McKinney spent the day at Mr. Van Doren's Sam is better Matt went to cousin Mary Nicholson's to spend the week.

5th   Went to see Aunt Ann, this evening, She had another cold coming on. Prayer meeting to night & last night. Concert of Prayer was had upwards of $30, raised for the different causes. Great excitement still about the sad state of the nation 7 states now out.

6th   Went this evening to see Mrs. Grant, Wilson, Tuttle, all quite well. Weather bright & mild.

7th   Went with cousin Mary to the Lunatic Asylum, in the evening to prayer meeting, more out than have been for some time.

8th   Matt came today. I at home all day to cousin Virginia's at night, with Matt, Mrs. Mc. & Mr. Curd.

9th   Today is sultry & damp. Miss Lizzie Scott & Sally Robertson here in the morning. I went to see aunt Ann a little while. John Stuart came, but brought the sad news that Sam was not going to Va.

10th   Raining hard this morning; I went to Sabbath school. 42 schollars, 2 female teachers. Mr. Marchmore preached. Had a thunder storm at night, no preaching therefore.

February 11th   Am going to-day with Mrs. McKinney to see about some company to Va. Oh! don't I hope I can go; just to be at home once more. Went to see about company; but it is very doubtful whether, they will go, will hear the last of the week.

12th   Went to Mr. Lawther's with cousin Martha, who spent the night here, to practice, staid there until 11 o'clock, then went to Dr. Abbott's, got stuck fast in the mud, had to cry aloud, for help. Charly Hockaday came to my relief pulled me out & put down a plank, to walk on. Aunt Ann much better; in the evening

Mrs. Mc. & myself started out to see if we could find some one going to Va., still uncertain. Went to prayer meeting at night.

13th Went to cousin Mary's to get her to write to cousin Mag Walkins to know about some one going to Washington, came home, quilted hard most of the day, at night crocheted, felt very sad, in fact took a cry, while Mr. Curd went to the office.

14th Riped my silk dress to fix over this morning. Some gentleman came to see Mrs. McKinney about the Arkansas suit nothing definite about it as yet. It has been raining & snowing all day. Went to the Methodist prayer meeting to night, felt it was truly good to be there oh! that I might be "as a City set on a hill, or as salt which has not lost its savor"

15th A bad day. No body coming in until late in the evening cousin Mary & Cally came up.

16th Mr. Wm George child funeral preached this morning good many went to the church expecting to hear it, but it was preached at the house. She was about 14 years old. Matt went to church. Mrs. McKinney to Mrs. Allen's I staid by myself. Matt & Mrs. Mc went to Dr. Abbott's in the evening. Mr. Hardin spoke to night.

17th Went to Church & Sunday school, full Sunday school. The Election of Deacons was made Mr. Tuttle & Dr. Overton were chosen. Mr. Marchmore preached at night on Prophacy. Very excellent.

18th Today is the Election, for candidates to the State Convention, the Union men have a large majority here. The affairs of the Nation still in distressed condition the peace conference at Washington, so far has accomplished but little. God help us in this the time of our need. Mr. Marchmore here in the afternoon; it is such a pity that he is so frivilous in his conversation, he is a true Christian, I believe but that is a weak point with him. No news of company to go home with me, oh! I do truly hope I can go. Very soon got two sermons from Richmond last night, by Mr. Wm. Reid & Mr. Mitchell one the National fast. Not read them yet.

February 19th Very unwell all day, feel so very weak. Matt went to see Mrs. Wm. George this evening, Mrs. McKinney to Dr. Karn's. I laid down, but was awaked by cousin Mary, Cally, Nancy & Matt Hockaday coming in. I soon got up. Later in the evening Miss Nancy Bragg & Tish Henderson came in, laid down again after all left, did not feel well enough to go to prayer meeting. Mr. Curd staid with me, Matt & Mrs. Mc went. Mr. Van Doren was there & prayed, he looks as if he had been near to Death's door, Sam Van Doren much better, Got a letter from home & from aunt Mary. No news of company home. Oh! can't tell how much I want to go.

20th   Weather Spring like, Mrs. Mckinney went to Mr. David Craigg's Matt to spend the night at Judge Henderson's I to see aunt Ann. Virginia Convention in Session, strongly Union, but I fear, there can be no compromise. Business stagnant every where, I am afraid the record of 1861, will be one of unprecedented sorrow should the glorious Republic be broken down. Make us to plead more at a throne of Grace for help.

21st   Matt came home this morning, weather very mild. I feel so badly just like in the Spring. Went to female prayer meeting six of us were there Mrs. Van Doren the first time for 8 weeks.

22nd   Mild & balmy. Matt went to Dr. Brewer's to have a tooth filled, & to cousin Sue's in the evening. Mr. Curd staid up some time after dinner. Mrs. James Robertson invited us to tea. I don't feel like going anywhere. I feel so terribly gloomy, this evening came thoughts in connection with the future almost overwhelm one, Oh! that I might become more reconciled to my *fate*. I feel as if I never could, I know it is wrong, I have so many blessings such a good home, kind husband who is never ceasing in his goodness to me, & the best of friends. Oh! that I might have the future in the hands of an all wise Creator, feeling that he will do best for me. All kinds of dark forbodings crowd into my mind this evening. I don't feel as if I could express my feelings to a mortal, & only write to try & find relief. Oh! God help me! Went to Mr. Robertson's, there were 16 or 18 persons there; there was one of the nicest kind of suppers set, of the greatest variety, but I had the most disagreeable evening. I couldn't shake off my distressing feelings, & besides had a *terrific* headache. Cousin Martha came home with Matt & spent the night.

23rd   Great changes in the weather this morning, windy & cold, went up to the house, to see about making some changes. Went to cousin Sue's in the evening to see Betty Nicholson, came home right soon, feeling dreadfully, laid down until supper. Matt staid to cousin Sue's until after supper, & from there went to sing-

ing school at the Methodist Church. Dr. Birch is to be the teacher.
Betsy came home with her, it has turned very cold, changes so
very sudden.

February 24th   Went to Sunday school, had a full and interesting
school. Was not well enough to go to Church. Staid at home & read
Alexander's Christian Experience.[10] Mr. Robert Dyer & Kate Coffman came home with Matt from church. Went to church at night.
Mr. Marchmore finished his lecture on Nebuchadnezzar's dream.

25th   Weather moderate but cloudy. Matt & myself promised to
go to Mr. Kerr's, but Mrs. K sent word he was not at home, wait
until Wednesday. Mite Society at Judge Bailey's.

26th   Mrs. Lawther, Watkins, Wilson & Miss Grant dined here
to-day, had a plesant day I thought. Mrs. Mckinney came home
this morning. Went to prayer meeting, good many out. Nothing of
encouragement relative to the future settlement of Federal
matters.

27th   Weather Bright & *warm* staid at home & quilted.

28th   Still warm, like May weather, the Day appointed by the
General Asembly for prayer for Colleges. Went to female prayer
meeting more there than usually is. Mrs. Van Doren came home
with me, she Mr. Van Doren's cousin Sue & Mr. Tuttle took tea
with us, & afterwards went to church, cousin S. not able to go, the
first time she has walked so far for some time. Mr. Marchmore
urged the subject of bringing up sons for the Ministry. There is a
Newspaper controversy going on between Mr. Laws & four Se-
niors, who were dismissed, for not informing on those who had
broken the rules or themselves, it is quite spicy, oh! What a pity it
should be thus. News came that the Critten Den compromise was
adopted.[11]

March 1st   Weather warm, was sitting quilting, rather sad in
feeling, when Mr. Curd came from the store, a thing so unusual,
all were surprised, he asked as soon as coming in if I could go to Va.
right away. I was too surprised to answer when he asked again, I
said no, not in two hours, then he told me Mr. Sam Dyer was going
on Monday & would take me to Washington, I bundled up & went
down town to get me a travelling dress, found one I wanted, came
home, cut it out & with much assistance got it done the next day
early.

March 2nd   Packed my trunk & was nearly ready to go, when a
note came saying Mr. Dyer could not go. I was not very much

disappointed, as they told me, he was fickle. I bore it bravely I thought. After some time Matt told me it was a hoax, (he Mr. Dyer) knew nothing of it, it was harder to make me think it a hoax, than, that he was not going. Went to see aunt Ann after dinner, & from there to cousin Sue's to supper. Cousin Mary Nicholson in town, came from cousin Sue's early, on account of its raining. Expect to start to Va. Monday, will not write more until I get home. Oh! to think of seeing home once more.

March 4th   Did not start to Va. to-day as expected. Mr. Dyer couldn't get off, was ready waiting for more than an hour. Matt & Mrs. Mc. went to see Henny, found her in bed with violent rheumatism. I sewed all day. Went to the house late in the evening, getting on slowly there.

5th   Stage came for me soon this morning, I had to hurry from breakfast, went down to Mr. Dyer's store, found he had not come from home, sent for, he then said he could not start as soon as the stage must go to meet the cars.¹² Mr. Curd got in with me, & Mr. Curtis said he would send Mr. D. on a swift horse, so he could overtake us. I felt quite uncertain about the matter, until he reached the stage, the roads dreadfully like riding over points, got to the river went over in the skiff, reached the depot, about 15 minutes before the cars came, had a safe trip to St. Louis, spent the night at cousin Thom Dyer's.

6th   This morning cousin Cornelia & I went to see cousin Mag Walker, her father is very feeble, don't think he will recover, came home expecting to start, in the evening didn't see Mr. Dyer until about seven o'clock, had a pleasant time in St. Louis.

7th   Started by light this morning, nothing unusual occurred to-day, arrived at Cincinnati, at nine o'clock to night, travelled all night.

8th   The usual routine of travelling in the cars. Met nor made no acquaintance everything & everybody seems prostrated by the distracted condition of the Country. Arrived at Wheeling about 10 o'clock (or Ben Wood). Went straight on Stopped at Grafton for dinner there I most unexpectedly met Dr. & Ned Parker. I felt glad to meet a familiar face from Richmond. Made a pleasant acquaintance from Kty a Dr. Todd he knew a number of Fulton people, travelled all night, arrived at the Relay House about 5 o'clock in the morning, changed cars.

9th 8th   Arrived in Washington about six o'clock, cousin Sam took me to the boat, put me under the care of the Capt., & bid me good bye, it was raining fast until we got near Richmond, when it cleared off. Arrived at Richmond half past 2 o'clock, the Capt. got me a hack, started for home just as I got a little above Breeden & Fox's saw Joe, knocked at him, he came across the street in perfect amazement little farther, saw father called him he was astounded, all went up together to the back gate surprised Betsy & Charlotte equally as much, felt quite fatigued had not changed my clothes since Thursday going day & night. Betsy told father to tell Mary to come up she wanted to see her, didn't tell her any thing until she came in the room and saw me, she could hardly believe it was I. Wrote to Mr. Curd directly I got here.

10th Was too fatigued to go out laid down most of the day. Sent for Marcella to come & stay with me she was sick in bed.

11th Went early this morning to see Mary Fox, staid a short time, from there paid a short visit to Lizzie Morton, she seemed as much pleased, as surprised to see me, from there to Marcella's found her better sitting up but with a very bad sore throat, spent the day with her. Aunt Jane seemed very bad, these times are enough to sadden any bodies heart, no better hopes for the Union, the State Convention & Legislature now in Session costing the State $2,300 daily is literally doing nothing, no hopes from Washington news. Had a number of calls yesterday, was sorry I missed them. Saw Mrs. George & the Brook's & Dr. Diane after I got back. Cousin Matt came down, but did not bring sister, am so sorry, it makes me fidgety because I can't see sister.

12th Father came from Court this morning, cousin Matt & Frank started home. It really is cold & wintry. Matt Durry came to spend the morning. Father, Betty & myself went to see cousin Barbara & Louisa in the evening. I was good deal fatigued when I came back, retired early.

13th Bright & mild, have had fine weather except part of a day since I left Mo. Wrote to Mr. Curd this morning want so much to see him. Betty & myself will go up to see sister this evening, how anxious I am to see her, felt quite badly all, laid down, Mary came up, & a little while afterwards Miss Nicholson came. I had to get up & dress, the last thing I felt like doing, went in & gave her the history of her brother's family, and away she went. While at dinner Molly Dandridge came, did not know we were going away; she rode down to the boat with us. When we got to the boat found

Dr. James & Thom Curd going up; father and Molly bid us good bye; the old Packet crawled off at a slow rate. We sat on deck until near supper time, was introduced to Mrs. Walter Leake; that honor of my sight Dick Watkins Esqr: was on the boat he talked every body out of patience. All sat together until the births were to be hung, the gentlemen took leave, *the Dr.* told Betty if he could awake he would see off the boat. At 12 o'clock Cedar Point was spied, off we went, the Dr. standing waiting to help us off. We went up to Mr. Pace's who keeps the house at the lock, as soon as shown our sleeping compartments, we went to bed, & though on no downy couch or satin spreads we slept none the less.

March 14th   The servant called us up in the morning, that Mr. Turner's carriage was waiting for us we hurried our rags on in hot haste arrived at Mr. Turner's about nine o'clock. All seemed glad to welcome us. Miss Caroline looked better then I expected to see her, spent the day pleasantly, rained hard in the evening. I took a rest, as I had no sleep on the boat.

15th   Went over this morning to see Col Anderson & Lady, saw Uncle Thom Curd there, the first time I had ever seen three such old people together, 81, 80, 76, was their respective ages; they had a great many questions to ask, about their Mo. kin & were gratified at seeing some one from there, sat several hours. Went back to Mr. Turner's. Sister came over that day & spent it at Mr. Turner's; in the evening all went over to her house; found all things as usual.

16th   Weather charming, Lucy, Betsy, John, Dr. John, Bet & Mr. Bowes, Mr. & Mrs. Turners, and Sally Turner spent the day with sister, it was pleasant to meet them all again, Betsy & Lucy spent the night.

17th   Cloudy, no Church to-day, every body stayed at home. Not long after breakfast, Sally Turner & Matt came over, they were looking well, they staid until after dinner, when all except Matt, went over to John's two in an open buggy, & the other in a spring wagon, it was raining fast, no body was hurt by it. - the roads were awfully bad.

18th   Very windy & cold, some snow, such a violent change. About 11 o'clock Joe came over in the buggy, & started over, Sally T. had been sick on the way but managed to get her to the house; she soon got well. Missy was over to meet us. James & all seemed well & everything looked just as it did when I left there. Snowed hard all evening and night. Real winter again.

March 19th Weather bright but quite cold, started to walk to Aunt Mary's, but was able to go no farther than the big gate, came back & laid down during the evening. Matt came for Sally and took her home this evening. Dre is in dreadful health.

20th Lucy, Betsy & myself went to Aunt Mary Ann's this morning. Aunt Mary looks about the same. Saw Bet Garland & her three children Oh! how desolate her situation, William was such a model husband; she had been at Aunt Mary's for some weeks. Bet Bowles' was over & spent the day. After dinner Sister & Betsy John came over & spent the night. Jinny gave us some sweet music after supper.

21st Went to Uncle Archer's this morning & from there to Archer Hart's, Lucy couldn't go as she was teaching school. James not well enough. left Betty John with her. Soon after dinner Nicy & Jinny came over, we staid a short time & then sister & myself, went up to Aunt Lucy's. Cold & windy. Aunt lucy like every body else was greatly surprised to see me, saw Pat Bolling there. Talked busily until bed time.

22nd Rose very soon this morning & went with cousin Matt to Bumpass' to take the cars, the roads were very rough. We got over half an hour before the cars came. Father came up as expected, told cousin Matt good bye & away we whirled, arrived at Keswick at 11 o'clock, walked to aunt Peggy's, she was so surprised to see me did not know me at first. In the evening Mag & cousin Fanny came over. Saw Jinny for a few minutes am sorry I can't see Fanny. Mag spent the night.

23rd Cloudy, cousin Susan & Mag went to the church to practice singing. Uncle James came over & took dinner. We went to Fruitland this evening. Mr. Robinson came from Amherst to-day nobody knows what he is aiming. All the family but one are at uncle James, the latter in bad spirits & health.

24th Clear & beautiful. Went to Walker's church, not many out, everything seems so cold & formal.

25th Weather still pretty, cousin Susan came over and dined to-day. Mag went with us to aunt Peggy's this evening to spend the night.

26th Father, aunt Peggy, Julia Magruder & myself, started to Uncle *Wms* this morning, arrived at North Garden Depot, -about 11, our letter had not been received saying we were coming, father went over to Thom Dew's place, & sent word from there that he &

three ladies were there. Uncle Wm. soon came over, was astonished to see me, as was Aunt Betty. Betty's children are so sweet' but I felt the absence of Betty & Andrew too much to enjoy my visit, -things had so sadly changed since I had been there. Betty's and Andrew's portrait are hanging in the parlor, so life like it seemed as if they must speak. Oh! the gloom which overhung every thing to me!!

27th   We had a heavy thunder storm this morning, with some hail, soon cleared off. Uncle Wm. Harris & wife came over & spent the day. Sent for cousin Angy, but she did not hear of it. Julia & myself had some pleasant chats together, she was much more pleasant to me than she used to be. Got a letter from Mr. Curd today. he had been quite unwell with his cold am so uneasy about that cold.

28th   All except Aunt Betty & Julia went to Uncle Wm. Harris to spend the day right soon this morning. Cousin Alfred & family were there, cousin A has three babies, it is such a charge for so delicate a person, her health is better than usual. She told me her Mother & Eliza were in Virginia, with Anna at present. Every thing in this neighborhood so still & quiet though much helped by the cars. When we got back to Sunny Bank, found Lilly Pinkerton there; she is much grown & so like her mother, is going to school at Mrs. Walter Coles & likes very much.

29th   Father & I left for Aunt Mary's this morning, first went to Charlottesville, stayed three hours nearly. Went to see Mrs. Dr. Carter & the Miss Leatmis & Betty Lewis, had a pleasant time talking over old times, & scenes. Left here about 12, for Stanton. Arrived there after 2 o'clock & took the stage for Midway, such times as we had, I thought I should have given out entirely, got to aunt Mary's after dark. She did not know I was in Va., but when I was asking Mr. Pinkerton if he did not know me, she called out *Sam* directly, was delighted to see both of us.[13] I laid down directly, ate no supper & soon as possible went to bed.

30th   Felt much better this morning, father had a sick headache all day. Aunt M. & I had quantities to talk about. She has six children with her & four boys boarding, a house full; but she takes every thing easily & quietly seems so happy. Midway is an ugly little place; but she says the people are very kind to her & quite nice.

31st   Lovely Sabbath, the church is in walking distance, so all went it is a very nice building & Mr. P. had a good congregation, he gave a plain practical sermon.

April 1st Cool & damp, I staid in doors, talking busily with aunt M. Father feels as if it is time for him to be going home, so quiet & little to be seen.

2nd Some ladies called to-day, I cut out a wrapping for aunt Mary, did not quite finish it, this is the last day with aunt Mary, I shall hate to say good bye: we talked until after eight, when all said it was time to fix for bed as we must be up soon after 12, to bed we went, but I slept little for fear I would not be up in time; was up and dressed before 1. The stage came quite soon & away we were packed in the horrid thing, had to ride all night, did not get to Stanton, until nearly six. I tell you I was tired enough.

April 3rd Left Stanton about 8 o'clock. It seemed almost a week, before we got to Richmond. I could hardly sit up. Betty did not look for us until thursday. Hoped to get Betsy Hart's likeness at Charlottesville, but aunt Betsy was sick & could not come to have it taken. Laid down & visited this evening, went to bed soon.

4th Feel much refreshed this morning, Marcella came up soon this morning. She is quite well, had a pleasant day. Cousin Ann Marie, Molly Dandridge & cousin Mary Fox came up in the evening. Cousin Matt came down to-day, Sister didn't say a word about coming, expect her next week. Heard from Mr. Curd yesterday he is quite well. Weather had been too cold to plaster the house.

5th Jobbed about this morning until late, when Betty & I went to Mrs. Brooks, found them as usual, busy sewing as if they had the world to clothe. chattered away briskly until about 2 o'clock, when we came home, father had come, & Dr. Gaines came soon after and took dinner with us; he is quite well, health seems to be much better. All well at Powhite, says Seaton makes himself ridiculous about his baby, Fanny is quiet about the matter.[14] He had just been to see Alice Carlton who is very low with consumption. Rode with him to the Lecture room, to prayer meeting. Had a pleasant meeting, it seemed so natural to be there, seeing so many familiar faces. After meeting, there was a general greeting of friends. Went over a little while to see cousin Elvira Grattard and Lucy, who were not well enough to be at church. From here went to Mary Fox's, took tea and sat until bed time, thus closed the program of the day.

6th   Cloudy this morning. Was disappointed in not seeing Mrs.
Gaines to dinner suppose Alice must be worse. Father saw Seaton
the rascal wouldn't come to see me. In the evening went to see
Mrs. Morton. She is terribly excited upon National troubles, saw
Molly's baby, a good looking child, I felt like an old grand mamy,
seeing *her baby*, it seems but as yesterday when she was most one
herself. Mr. Hobson's health no better. Came back by Mrs.
Crump's poor woman, what a shame she married Smith, such a
sacrifice of herself. Got a long, nice letter from Matt, things going
on as usual in Fulton. Was so sorry to hear that Mr. Curd's cold
was no better, am so uneasy about it.

7th   Raining all day, did not go out at all, read most of the day,
was anxious to hear Mr. Read.

8th   Raining hard all night and day, looks like the long season in
May, wish it would clear off, want to see so many people. Father
gone to Caroline Court, Betty and I busy talking, if Sister were
with us 'twoud' be so nice.

April 9th   Raining as hard as ever, father came home today.
Heard from Mr. Curd last night, they are having rain enough
there now, more than has fallen in two years. His cold is better, all
were well. The Country still in the highest state of excitement. No
business done.

10th   Rained hard all day, this is the 5th day, which has caused a
great freshet, the bridges are washed away, no mail coming in.
James River is so high as to be some distance up on the lumber
houses at Rocketes, and boats are rowing, down all around the
basin. Mr. Curd writes there has been a great deal of rain in
Missouri.

11th   Was glad to wake and see the sun shining brightly, twas
truly cheering, everybody has been so weather bound they were
like loosed birds, out in gangs. Betsy and I went out early, first to
see Mrs. George, from there to Lizzie Morton's, found the latter
quite unwell, has an infant, little girl, about 4 weeks old, this is her
5th child, it seems most impossible spent some time with her, and
from there went to see Marcella, found her sick again, spent the
day with her and would have staid the night, but later came for me
to go and see Mrs. Gaines, went up and found her quite well. She
spent the night, and of course we had lots to chat about. Told me
all about Fanny and the baby which is nearly two months old, it
seems so strange to think of Fanny and Seaton with a baby, it is

named Hatty. Molly Dandridge spent the night here. Not a word of sister yet.

12th. Weather threatening again. Mr. Seaton Linsley came for Mrs. Gaines very soon this morning, Molly went home, Betty and I to see cousin Celia and Sally Dyer, had a long talk over their Mo. kin. Went to see Mr. Read and family, all out but Mrs. R, she as busy as ever with society work, reports her Sunday school as doing well. I used to have a class in it, she attends to the infant-department. Then went to see Mrs. Hiram Smith, was sorry I had so short a time to stay; but had promised Mary Fox to dine with her and it was then 1 o'clock. We told her goodbye, promising to come and spend the day very soon. After this to Mary's where we staid until nearly night. Had come home in the rain. Things still distressing in the Nation. What is to be done the wisest can't discern, Lincoln's policy is decidedly secret. Poured in rain all night.

13th. Poured in torrents this morning until eight o'clock, when it cleared off partially, so windy did not go out until very late went down to Mrs. Blairs. News came this evening that Fort Sumpter has been taken by the South Carolinians, greatest excitement, amounting almost to a Mob; tonight, pulled down the Stars and Stripes off the Capitol, and raised the Secession flag, had a torch light procession &ᶜ Truly evil days have fallen on us. None can say what the future will be for us. The people seem most mad.15

15th. The day bright as possible; went to the Infant S.S. this morning quite a number of little ones there, and seemed to enjoy singing their hymns very much. Heard Mr. Read preach in the morning, went to Mary Fox's to dinner, and in the evening to Church again. Mr. Terhune preached.

16th. Somewhat cloudy, staid in all morning, Mrs. Crump, (alias Mrs. Smith) came in, the exciting times the whole subject of talk, Lincoln has issued proclamation, for the border states to send in their quota of men to fight for the North, of course it was received with great indignation and every body in the highest state of excitement. God save us in this time of our great necessity. Went to Dr. Gaines in the evening, Fanny looks wretchedly and has no energy. Dr. G. started to Presbytery to-day. Everything is most washed away.

17th. Rained hard last night and this morning, all went over and spent the day with Sally, it seemed like old times. Mr. Gaines came to Richmond, and came back bringing such gloomy news, it made one truly sad, Oh! I am so anxious to be with Mr. Curd, hope to see him soon.

18th.   Cloudy in the morning, but cleared off, staid until 12 o'clock with Sally and then came home. Saw some gentlemen on the streets who gave us some startling news, it seemed as if war was upon us, the military all making preparation to go at a moments call. Dr. Gaines came back as the port of Norfolk, was being blockaded, it is awful to think of Civil War.

19th.   April weather, sunshine, and shower. Mrs. Smith and Vic called today. Went to Marcella's this evening, she quite unwell. Aunt Jane much distressed about the times. Sent for to come and see sister, hurried home, she never saw such roads all day, nearly, coming. Cousin M & Frank came with her. "Virginia *seceded* today."[16]

20th.   Cousin Matt went off this morning; every body in the greatest state of excitement. Mails & telegraph stopped between here and the North. News came that a company from Boston, were attacked in Baltimore, some killed and 20 wounded. It was a most daring attack; the company passed on to Washington. I shall be undone won't hear from Mr. Curd.

April 21st.   Bright and lovely day. Went to church in the morning. Everybody seems so thoughtful and troubled. As we came back to-day the bells tolled for the summoning of the companies; it sounded as if twere the death toll of the Nation. All were in great distress having (as they thought,) to bid good bye, perhaps forever with those who were dear and near to them. It was one of the most distressing days I ever experienced. But it was all false alarm, the companies were disbanded at night and we welcomed Joe Anderson, feeling almost as if he had resurrected.

22nd.   Sister went down to see cousin B- I staid at home and very soon Mrs. Narcissus Miller came. She like every body else was much distressed at the condition of things. Uncle Thom came this morning, and then came and spent the night. He has grown so very deaf.

23rd.   Today is warm, makes me feel real spring like. went down to see Lizzie Morton so warm I spent the day. Sally Gaines came in with Mr. Gaines, his company has been ordered here. We went to the Fair ground where they all, are encamping, said he had soldiers ration which was old beef and a piece of bread. All said she bore the idea of his coming mighty well. Fanny unwell, and very low-spirited about Seaton's joining the companies. About 700 soldiers from different places came in to-day.[17] Heard yesterday from Mr. Curd the letter had been a long time coming.

24th.   Went down to Mary's, to get her to help me make some soldiers shirts, the ladies all around town are helping make them uniforms, the whole country South seem aroused in defiance of Lincoln's proclamation, oh! the great distress which will be brought upon us. God help us and strengthen our faith. The Convention declared Virginia, as belonging to the Southern Confederacy April 24th. 1861.[18] Maryland has come out nobly in defence of the South, has called her Legislature, and will no doubt follow Va. I am so anxious to hear from Mr. C-

25th.   Cousin Matt and Mr. A, who came down yesterday, went back this morning Frank went with them. Nothing new in the way of Military operations. Major Lee, has been made General of the forces of Virginia, which is universally approved. A number of the soldiers are in camp.

26th.   Nothing of any especial interest occurred to-day.

27th.   Weather warm but so dusty you can scarcely see. I went to Mrs. Durry and sat some time, from there to Mrs. George; but had not been there but a few minutes before they sent for me, telling me Sally and Fanny Gaines had come in, I hurried off, and found them waiting to take me to the New Fair Grounds to see Mr. Wm. Gaines who is in camp out there. Had a most dusty ride, he was being drilled, the Cadets are there making squads of 5 and 6 drill at a time. Every thing looks like War Preparation it made my heart sad to see it. When we got back I rode with Sally down as far as Marcella's, and staid there until nearly dark.

28th.   The weather bright but terribly dusty and windy, went to church twice. Sally came back with Mr. Gaines who had permit to go out and spend the day and night.

29th.   Sister went to the church to help make soldiers clothes. I was not well enough to go, Sally spent the day at the Baptist Institute. Joe was lying down has boil on his leg which prevents his drilling with the Howitzers. Betty & I staid at home.

30th.   Mrs. George came by for me to go up & see the South Carolina soldiers, found most of them such gentlemen, seemed to be from the nicest families, & brought from home only to fight because they felt they had been oppressed. Weather very bluster-

ing. Dr. Gaines called on his way to see Mr. Gaines. I was very
unwell all day taken quite sick about night had to send for Dr.
Deans. Marcella here in the evening. Heard from Mr. Curd the
letter had been coming 7 days.

May 1st.   Was in bed all day. Nothing of any interest about the
things pertaining to the Country. Weather so cool, the soldiers
must suffer at night.

2nd.   Dry, bright & windy, had company all day, am up, but feel
very weak. Sally went to spend the day and night with Lizzie Morton. Cousin Matt came down. Sad times to every body, a gloom
seems to be spread over the Whole Community. Oh! I am so anxious to have Mr. Curd with me, wish we could all be together these
troubleous times. My only hope is in God. May I have grace to do
my part.

3rd.   To-day one year ago we were married, Oh! the changes
which this short period had made; then all was prosperity & peace,
now the whole Country is in a distracted state, the North arrayed
against the South. Railroads, Telegraphs &c broken up for general
use. I now hear the beating of the drums for drill, where before
nothing of the kind was ever heard. What the next year may bring,
is in mercy veiled from our eyes. Sister & cousin Matt went home
this morning am so sorry; hoped sister would stay until I went.
Cool & cloudy Sally came back this evening with Dr. Linsley, I
think he must lead a rather dissipated life from his looks, he has no
idea of joining any of the companies. Went to Mrs. Brooks.

4th.   Raining a little this morning. Mr. Gaines came in from his
encampment quite soon, had permit to stay until Monday morning. Betty went with them to have their daguerotype & hers
taken, all right good, did not see Sallie's. They went home this
evening. I staid at home father & Betty went to the Fair Ground to
see the S. Carolinian's drill, in dress parade. I could hear the music
from here it was very fine. Very cool.

5th.   Morning bright, Betty went to S. School. I did not go out
during the day not well enough. Raining in the evening; but father
& Betty went out to Communion Service. I was so sorry I could
not go, was so anxious to commune once more in our church, as it
is uncertain when I may ever be here again; but it was otherwise
ordered. Am so anxious to know about Mr. Curd.

6th.   Raining this morning, & most of the day, felt so depressed, saw part of the Howitzers come by they were ordered to

West Point. Joe came up in great hurry to be ready to go as he did not know which would be sent. Oh! it is so sad to think of the flower of our Country being led to the battle field. 700 Louisianians came in tonight, arrivals constantly. Had a powerful rain this evening & tonight, like washing every thing away.

7th. Father & Lewis went to the New Fair grounds to get Willy Hart's clothes, he has contracted a cold which prevents his going with his company & I am afraid will settle on his lungs. Spent the day with Mary found her gone to the church when I got there, to sew for the soldiers. Father's company the Home Guard, mustered this evening it seems strange to see such old men turn out soldiering. Joe did not go off as he thought he might do.

8th. Not very well laid down in the morning. Dressed to take a walk, just as we were about to start Marcella came in & all went to the Old Fair Ground, parade was almost over, saw plenty of people stayed a short time & came home. Betty & father went to Wednesday night lecture, Marcella & I stayed here. The S. Carolina band played most delightfully, one piece Listen to the Mockingbird excelled any thing I ever heard.

May 9th. Weather bright & beautiful. Marcella would go home. Betty was busy making something to send Joe a snack. In the evening I went to Mary's a little while & from there to Lizzie Mortons, & then to Marcella's to spend the night. Surprised to find aunt Lucy there had just come down, Betty & father went with me father left directly after supper to go to drill. Aunt Jane very unwell. Crilly Hart's looks shocked me he is more altered than I could imagine any body could be in a few weeks, poor fellow consumption seems to have marked him for a victim, I don't think he will live six months if he don't improve, how sad to see one so young thus stricken, & oh! saddest of all entirely without hope. Great God convert him.

10th. Felt quite well when I first got up, was taken strangely sick in a few minutes, & had to go to bed stayed there several hours; father came for me about 1, o'clock took me home. rainy day. Aunt Lucy & John Hope spent the night with us. Father had to go out & stand guard, he hated it very much but did not feel as if he should shrink from it, the Home Guard with the regular City Guard are all out to prevent the setting houses on fire & other depredations as there have been a number of fires within a few days. Mary up here this evening. Joe came down from his "camp,"

& spent the morning he likes as well as he expected. Expected to be on guard next day.

11th. Things move on as usual. Heard from Mr. Curd this evening, he has been quite sick, too much so to come for me, feel so uneasy about him. Oh to be with him once more I shall be so delighted.

12th. Not well enough to go to church. Wrote to Mr. Curd, telling him if he was well enough I wanted him to come if not I would go on with Mr. Marchmore, who expects to be at the General Assembley, in Philadelphia. I expect they will have hot times don't suppose the Southern members will go.

13th. Father went to Court to-day. I was not up until 9, O'clock, weather bright & quite warm, walked up to the Garden in the evening. John Anderson came while were at supper. Garland here yesterday, he belongs to the Goochland troop, looks so handsome in uniform. Thom & little Matt both in that company.

May 14th. Marcella went home soon. I walked with her as far as Mr. James Thomas. Sister, Lucy & cousin Matt came at 1, o'clock, came down in Carry all. Was so glad to have them here. After dinner John, Betty, Lucy & myself, went together in a hack to Howard Grove, where the Howitzers are stationed, to see Joe, it is a lovely place, but they have to move in short time; Joe well & in very good spirits. Sister & cousin Matt went with uncle Wm. in their Store wagon. From here we went up to the New Fair ground, to see dress Parade, there are a large number of soldiers here, & a great many spectators this evening but it made my heart sad to think what all this was for. So many young men & men of families, who are of promise to be cut down by the ruthless sword. Father did not get home until night, the cars detained on some Military purpose, for which all things subserve now.

15th. Sister & the rest went home this morning. It makes me peculiarly sad to say good bye such times as these. Oh! I am so anxious about Mr. Curd am so afraid he will not be well enough to come for me. Being from him so long weighs upon my mind all the time. Mary Dandridge, Massy Anderson & Shelton who is just from Louisiana after an absence of 12 or more years, came to see us, the latter has so very much improved & looks like a twin brother to Garland. He reports the South as being en masse for fighting. Lucy & Lizzie Gratran came while they were. Lizzie said Mr. Stiles & sons had come, the latter to fight for Va. Had a bad cry this evening about *my situation*. Oh! that I might become reconciled, & not murmur; but think how much worse it might have been. Father & Betsy went to Wednesday night lecture, could not walk so far. Mary up here this morning. Julia has diptheria, not a bad case.

16th. Mary Massy spent the night here, father went to drill, feeling quite badly, and so anxious about Mr. Curd, if he would only come, may I never be so situated again.

17th. Aunt Betsy sent me the likeness of Betty & Andrew to have copies taken. Sally Gaines & the Dr. came in to the [name unreadable] Synod which met yesterday, this body is free of all Yankee troubles a quite good number for the times present. Rode down town to see about Betty's likeness & from there to the New Fair Ground to see the dress parade. It is truly a sight, but one that makes my heart bleed to see such preparation for killing people. Believing we are in the right, I trust we shall be blessed. Troops are constantly coming in. Wm. Henry came & spent the night. Most of them went to church. I shall have to be debarred the privilege of going as it is too far to walk.

18th. Oh! I feel so awfully depressed, every thing seems so gloomy, & I feel particularly so, separated from Mr. Curd, & not hearing how he is. Wm. Henry Harris, Dr. Gaines & Mrs. Gaines spent the night here.

19th. Bright early, but grew cloudy. All went to church but myself, was very unwell all day. Mr. Stiles preached this morning was anxious to hear him, communion in the evening. Blessed privilege Christians have, while all around is excitement, to be permitted to retire & hold united converse with God.

20th. Betty went to the church to help sew for the soldiers. A regiment from Tenessee came to the Old Fair Ground. Mary came up & staid until after dinner.

21st. Spent the morning quietly with Sally Gaines in the evening went to the Old Fair Ground. They are a rough looking set of men, but look as if they were ready to fight. Mr. Richard Gaines came with Mr. Wm. & spent the evening.

22nd. Nothing of any variety today. Not a word from Mr. Curd yet, it is so strange. Mr. Gaines came to night, & told Sally he was ordered to leave the next morning, poor woman, it is so sad to see such separation, she has had so far great fortitude, he spent the night with her.

23rd.   Dr. Gaines in soon this morning, all went to the Fair ground stayed a little while & came back for Sally's baggage, she looked decidely "blue", went home this morning. I went to Mary's this evening & spent the night. Betty & Matt & Mr. George Denny went to the New Fair ground to tell some soldiers who will leave to-morrow good-bye. Father & Betty spent the evening with me at Mary's, the latter spent the night.

24th.   Betty went to the church again today. I spent the day with Mary. Every thing this evening in the greatest excitement so many companies leaving, I feel peculiarly depressed. Got papers from Mo & no letters. I can't account for not having a letter. Mary & Father walked home with me this evening.

25th.   Was glad to have Joe with us until after dinner, was afraid he had been ordered off. Staid at home all day. Weather warm & very dry. No tidings yet from Mo terrible suspense.

May 26th.   Was again surprised to have a visit from Joe, staid all day. Seems to be in good spirits & has fattened. Went with me to the Grace Street church. Very warm all day. He went back to camp not long before dark. Large numbers of soldiers sent to Manassa Gap yesterday & a few days previous. The Federal Troop have taken possession of Alexandria. A Col. was shot by a Hotel keeper for taking down S. Confederate flag, he was in turn cut to pieces by the Federal soldiers No action has yet taken place only a few skirmishes—this was written on Tuesday (not Sunday).

27th.   Marcella came up some this morning, & staid all day & night. The most dusty, blustering day I ever saw. Dust settles on every thing have to keep doors & windows shut. Willy Hart went with his company to Manassa Gap.

28th.   Joe came up again to-day & spent the day am so glad his company have not left. Military preparations going very rapidly, there is no telling when action will begin. Betty went down to try & get me a common dress; but every thing had been sold out, or marked high. I am entirely with out thin clothing, & each day seems an age, as I cant hear from, or see Mr. Curd. No letter from him since the date May 2nd. I know he must write; it is so distressing to be thus.

29th.   Very unwell most of the day, laid down until 12, o'clock, Betty had a nice snack of black berry wine & a hot muffin with some chipped veil, which refreshed me. But oh me I cant enjoy any thing as I would under any other circumstances. I have looked so

long to hear & see Mr. C. only to be disappointed, that I feel perfectly down cast. Wont I have lots to talk to him about when we
meet once more. I hope never to be separated from him so long
again. President Davis arrived here this morning. Great enthusiasm on the occasion. Congress will meet here in July, as this is the
chosen seat of Government. I trust it may never be so demoralizing as the former one was. 13th. June appointed as a fast day by the
President. All alone to night, father & Betty gone to church. If it
would be any relief to my feelings I could write all night.

    30th.   Wrote to Mr. Curd to-day doubt if he ever gets it. Mrs.
Smith here in the evening, nothing new of interest.

    31st.   Joe came up this day, Mary Fox here in the evening. I had
a *big cry*, couldn't hold in, didn't tell Joe or Mary good bye. Father
went to drill to-night.

    June 1st., 61   I cant realize that the year has so far advanced, &
what great changes have happened, every thing seems turned out
of its usual course. Betty complaining, I sewed on the flounces of
her Verage dress. Aunt Jane & cousin Barbary here this evening,
found Betty & myself stretched out on the lounge. Aunt J has not
heard from Willy Hart.

    2nd.   Went to the 3rd church. Mr. Jeter gone away on account
of Mrs. Jeter's bad health. Betty & Joe went with me, the latter up
all day. Cousin Matt came down to-day. Sister & Uncle Archer had
been up to see Fanny heard no news about their visit.

    3rd   Betty & cousin Matt went out this morning to see Joe, I
think it probable his company will stay here. Mary Dowden had a
boy last night, her next to the youngest only *13 months* old, she is to
be pitied. Father has gotten a place for Lewis, at the Spottswood
House.[19] I don't often like to see into the future, but would like to
know if Mr. C is not coming this week. Damp & cloudy, had a
heavy rain this evening. Betty father & myself took a walk after
supper, the air cool & refreshing. Had been in but a little while,
when Joe came up, he had been ordered to leave next morning
came to say good bye. Oh! I am so sorry he is going, it is distressing
to tell him farewell, so many young & promising young men thus
snatched from their homes it is indeed distressing. We can only
commit him & them all into the hands of God. Oh! What a year this
will be to all!!—The Howitzers are to join their other company at
Yorktown. The Federal troops are pillaging every thing they can
without regard to sex, or value. Families near Hampton are leav-

ing in secrecy, taking scarcely the necessaries of life. Such times seem incredulous to believe them.

4th   Cloudy & damp, I making a 12½, its lawn, have no summer clothes with me, but this is nothing to the distress of mind I feel about Mr. Curd. I feel at times as if I must sink under it. Betty at church all day sewing. Mary came up in the evening, Joe did not go until late to night. It rained hard all night am afraid he will get sick. Nothing new about matters.

5th   Cloudy & raining fine, most of the day, accords with my feelings. Father heard from Uncle Wm. Hart, said Wm. A. & Markon were in Washington & Alexandria still, heard very little from them. I can't imagine why they did not join a company or leave poor aunt Julia, every body has their trouble now.

June 6th, 7th & 8th   Nothing of any importance occured. I still feel wretchedly as no tidings from Mr. Curd.

9th   Bright & pleasant. Col. Parker came in & sat a little while in the porch. Saw a regiment of soldiers go down Franklin; they are on lend to Phillipi. I went to the 3rd Church too far to walk to Mr. Reid's. Mrs. Harding & Mrs. Jeter came up this evening & sat with me. She tried to cheer me but it is the suspense which is so hard to bear, not knowing where, or how he is. Heard the Howitzers had been ordered from Yorktown, to Bethel Chapel, where was expected to be a battle. God preserve their lives.

10th   A terrible Battle was fought today as expected.[20] There were 4000 Federalist against 800 Confederates, & yet the latter gained a great victory, the former retreated, with 450 killed & a number not known wounded; but one of our men killed & 3 wounded. What a signal display of the working of Providence that each heart might recognize. it. All accounts report almost unknown bravery on the part of our men. A.N.C. company was in the engagement who acted most nobly.

11th   Betty went to the church to sew. Sally Gaines sent up to know if I had heard from Mr. Curd, but I had to give the same old answer. Got a letter from Joe, but it was written before the battle, he was well but had not had a chance to change his clothes for nearly a week.

12th   Mrs. Gaines & Sally came in this morning before I was up, brought in Mr. Gaines who had been up several days. He was well Sally bears her troubles with the greatest fortitude. They persuaded me to go out with them all thought some change would do me good. We had a *hot* ride out, but the country looked so beautiful & refreshing. I felt the change was pleasant. Fanny & baby gone to Mrs. Linsley's.

13th   The day passed quietly without any interruption.

14th   Sally & I went to Fairfield to see about some of her housekeeping matters. Mrs. Gaines made a visit to Dr. Curtis, she brought back two soldiers shirts, which we finished that night.

15th   Very warm, & I have the deepest blues, such bad news from Mo, I am afraid Mr. Curd will be kept away. Helped to make two soldiers jackets.

16th   I was sleeping this morning not having rested well for several nights, was awakened by Mrs. G coming in. I saw she had a yellow envelope in her hand. She gave it to me, but I was so excited I had to give it to Sally to read. What was my delight to hear that Mr. C would be here in a day or two oh how thankful I am. Telegraph came from Tenesee. Father came out as soon as he got the dispatch he spent the day.

June 17th   Father & I came home soon this morning, every thing quiet here. Harper's Ferry is said to be evacuated, for purposes known only to the Commanders. Betty went to the church to sew. I went to see Mrs. Crump in the evening & from there to Mary Fox's where all took tea. Oh! I feel like a different creature, since getting that dispatch. Heard from sister while I was gone. She is very much depressed & since cousin Matt's overseer has gone he is so confined she cant come down; wish she was here.

18th   Warm & dusty. Good news!! Mr. Curd got here to day about 2, o'clock, he was not at all detained on the way, but had been looking for me every day to come with Mr. Marchmore. As soon as he heard he had come without me he started off at a moments notice. He is very unwell & looks wretchedly has still a bad cough. Am so thankful he has come.

19th   Nothing of interest happened today. Oh! yes, had a number of arrivals. Ella, & aunt Mary Ann came down with Matt Archer, & after dinner cousin Wm. A. Hart came, he staid in Alexandria some time after the Federalist took possession, they injured, & robbed his store quite extensively, & says they commit all sorts of depredations. Marion is still in Washington.

20th   Excessively warm. Seaton Linsley came in a little while this evening, said Sally & Fanny were both very complaining, & had an ill servant. News from Missouri is 1st the Federalist had taken possession of Jefferson, & another report is that Lyon who

is Commander of the whole Federal force, had been taken prisoner
at Boonville, too good I'm afraid to be true. Oh! What an awful
condition our whole land is in. God bring us salvation for vain is
man.

21st   Very warm all night & this morning. Thom Curd came
down he belongs to the Goochland Artillery. Mr. C. had gone out.
Ella & them went out this morning. Uncle Wm. Hart came to day,
he is perfectly furious about the Yankees, & talks in his usually
extravagent style. Mr. Curd very unwell, though we walked down
to Mary's after tea, it is still warm.

22nd   Went over to Mrs. Brooks a little while this morning,
have everything packed to start to Mo Monday. Oh! I wish it suited Mr. C to stay in Va, the dear spot, & these such times I feel like
all being together, but I trust I shall be sustained by an Almighty
Arm. Father is very uneasy about my going back, is afraid we will
have trouble by the way, & then not be safe after getting there. It
is such bad times to say good bye to them all, when we will again
meet, God only knows. Poor Betty she says she will miss me as
much as when I left at first, it is a pity a young girl should have
cares, so much, it makes them prematurely old. Cousin B, Marcella
Louisa, & Molly came this evening. We had quite a Levee after tea,
friends coming to say good bye, all anxious for fear it will not be
safe for us to go. We have no ice this summer of course suffer for
it, after all had left tonight, we walked up to the well on two
squares alone for some water. This is the last night but one, for me
to stay at my dear home! Oh me!

23rd   All went to church but Mr. Curd & myself, I put on my
dress, & found it not fit to make my appearance in. Dr. Diane came
about 11 o'clock had a long chat about the matters of the day, &
gave me all sorts of advice. Very warm. Mary Fox & Mr. F & children came in, also letters sent in to be mailed by us, as no mail is
now made up in the Seceded States, for the United States. Went to
tell Mrs. Crump good bye. Mr. & Mrs. Reid came in & sat a little
while after tea. Nearly every body has been in to see me. Betty
went with us up stairs & sat with us little while, oh it is so hard to
leave them, I can scarcely restrain my feelings. I wrote to sister but
she said they were harvesting & cousin Matt could not leave as
Mr. Cullivan is in the Army, so I will not see her am so *very sorry* for
it. I scarcely slept at all, & arose disturbed & but little refreshed. I
couldn't describe my feelings.

24th   Uncle Wm. & cousin Wm. Andrew both go off this morn-

ing, wish sister was here, Betty would miss me less, she says shes
going to the church every day & work hard for the soldiers. Got
up, every thing ready, went to tell Ann good-bye & see Charlotte a
little while breakfast came, the hack came & off we all started for
the Depot; Betty & father sat a little while with me in the Cars, but
I was too full, to talk much, after the last good bye from them
came, how hard to bear oh! these separations are terrible to stand,
the cars whistled & off we started. Mr. Hooper came up very soon
& spoke to me, he was going to Lynchburg. It was warm & drissly,
nothing of note happened during the day, stopped at Lynchburg
for dinner, Betty had a snack for me, so we ate that. Got to Liberty
late in the evening, traveled all night.

June 25th   Traveled all day very warm & dusty good many people on board. I did not expect to see a lady travelling such times,
very warm & dusty though the crops look good. Arrived at Chat-
tanooga to supper, changed cars, the cars were filled, & they had
these high up seats, which I found very uncomfortable, I scarcely
slept until nearly day took a nap. Mr. Curd not well still coughs.
I'm so uneasy about him. Saw a number of Soldiers going to Virginia. This road is terribly rough it is through the mountains of Tenesee & Virginia, as we are in the Confederate States found all
agreed in political matters.

26th   Arrived at Nashville this morning about 9, o'clock very
warm & as we had not washed since Monday were sights to be
seen, stopped at the St. Cloud, the rooms were plain, but the fare
very good. I enjoyed a bath exceedingly & after changing my
clothes we took a nap. Mr. Curd laid down, but did not sleep it was
so warm. Staid here until 3, o'clock train, when we started for
Louisville, arrived at Louisville about 12 o'clock, had been detained
by a slight accident, which made us loose the regular connection,
but we went on to Seymour & got there about light, I don't think I
ever was so tired and sleepy in my life, this was the third night,
without sleeping, just what we could in our seats. We went to a
tavern couldn't say hotel, & laid down as soon as possible & slept
almost 3 hours. I felt very differently after waking.

27th   We took the Ohio & Mississippi road at 9, o'clock very
few on board. No body talking on the subject of the times, I should
of course have been obliged to be Mum. Saw one Federal officer on
board. There was quite an encampment across from St. Louis, it
made me feel awful to see them. Arrived at St. Louis about 9,

o'clock at night took supper as soon as possible, wrote part of letter home, as I found a gentleman coming out who said he would send a letter from Louisville to be mailed South; they will be so glad to get it as all feared we would have much trouble getting out here, but there never was a more quiet trip taken. I went to bed as soon as possible had a good night's rest & felt refreshed next morning. St. Louis looks as if people had gone to take holiday.

June 28th   Morning cloudy & raining when we started for St. Aubert. I was glad as we had, had such dry, dusty time before. We came up on the Pacific as the bridge had been repaired, but the whole road was guarded by Dutch Soldiery, it was tantalizing to see them. Jefferson City has been taken by the Dutch & one of the most notorious of the Dutch Scamps has been placed at the head of affairs every body there has to submit or leave the place.[21] Mo is truly in a bad fix. No arms & Federal troops pouring in upon her. Oh! what a distressed condition is our Nation in nothing but war & destruction starring us in the face. We had a comfortable ride to St. Aubert; had to cross the river in a sciff the sun pouring down at the rate of 90°. The Federalist had taken the Ferry boat for their purposes. Found the roads from St. Aubert very bad, got to Fulton after dark, found Matt all alone, had expected us that night, she seemed delighted that Mr. Curd had not been taken prisoner or killed or some thing bad had not happened to him. Mrs. McKinney had gone to Mr. Lawther's who has had his leg hurt by a horse kicking him. In a few minutes Mr. Marchmore made his appearance, we had quite a talk on Succession & Union.

29th   Day very rainy, so much so no body came in until after night Fanny Barbour came over. Mr. C. very unwell.

30th   Did not go out to day. Mrs. Watkins here in the evening. Mr. Curd went to see Mr. Lawther he is no better.

July 1st   Went soon this morning to the house was surprised there was so much to be done. Had company all day every body congratulatd us, as if we had escaped the fiery furnace, I felt gratified at their manner. Mr. C says he never was so welcomed home.[22] We should be truly gratified for our safe journey in these perilous times.

2nd   Still had calls, did nothing else but entertain today. Miss Agnes Bristoe, & Sally Robinson, & Mr. & Mrs. Strong dined here, & cousin Sue, Mr. & Mrs. S will leave this week for good. The College is in such condition that it is not paying its professors.

Went to Mr. Lawthers this evening after all left. he is confined to his bed. We had high talk about National Matters he as strong Union as I am Secessionist.

3rd   Nothing of importance heard of or done. I am ripping up old dresses trying to make them new.

July 4th 1861   What a contrast is afforded in this days celebration from those of former years. United states Congress meets to day. The whole land in distress, nothing but awful forebodings of the future. The South arrayed in deadly conflict against the North Oh! distressing! a wagon full of ladies & gentlemen, Matt among the number went out picnicing trying to at least keep past honor of the day. They reported having a pleasant day. There was quite a conflict as to whether Dixie, or Star Spangled Banner should be sung. Dixie gained the day, hurrah!

5th   Day passed off quickly, one would never imagine that war was going on in the land, from the quietude which reigns. God in his mercy keep us thus through the whole course of events; how long it may be the case I cant say. but I try to feel, "sufficient unto the day is the evil thereof."

6th   Busy mending up Mr. Curd's clothes & getting things generally straight. Very warm; but we have plenty of ice, what my dear father & Betty with the rest of Virginia have not. I use it thinking of them.

7th   Warm again at first thought I could not go to church, but then felt, I was doing wrong probably & ought to make a sacrifice of my feelings & go, so I did, but it was a trial. Mr. C hates for me to feel this way. Went again at night. Mr. Marchmore preached both times, if he was not to light & undignified it would improve him so much.

8th   Very warm. Staid in doors all day Mrs. Abbott spent the morning here, had not heard from Aunt Ann since she left Mr. Nicholson, am so sorry I couldnt see her. Heard from Mr. Lawther, they found out yesterday evening his leg was broken, it seems strange Dr. Scott did not see it sooner. Dr. Abbott discovered it; it has been 4 weeks since it was done. Matt & myself went with Mrs. Barbour & Miss Fanny to Dr. Harrison's had only tolerable times. Mrs. Mc went to see Mr. Karns. Awfully oppressive, but had a storm about 11 o'clock which cooled the atmosphere.

9th   Everything went on as usual, very warm still.

10th   Mrs. McKinney went to the country with Miss Bristoe to

Mr. Robinson's; she is unusually melancholly; has enough to make her so.

11th Feeling very unwell all day, but managed to keep up, helped Matt make a white swiss body striped with [word unreadable], it is pretty.

July 12th Felt dreadfully this morning. Hetty Monroe spent the night with Matt & as soon as she left I laid down, after a little while Mrs. Jemerson came for Matt to go with her to see Miss Patton, I insisted she should go, while gone Mrs. Abbot came, I grew more unwell, & about 11 o'clock began to vomit which I continued to do until 11 o'clock at night. Nothing quieted me in the least; & with it had violent pains. Dr. Abbott thought I would have premature sickness;[23] but I fortunately escaped & got easy enough about 11, to fall into a dose. Cousin M staid all night, also the Dr.

13th Very weak & faint all day, had to keep very quiet all day, company came all day, but I didn't do any talking. Preaching at the Presbyterian Church to-day. Cousin Mary Nicholson came in this morning, Mr. Curd staid with me & Matt went with her to church services preparatory to communion; but the church seems to be so engrossed in the present state of affairs as to be blind to that very thing which might, & *only* can, give her comfort.

14th Cousin Mary staid here all night, Mr. Curd staid with me while they were gone to church feel better, sat up a little while but am very weak, communion today.

15th Some one in & out all day, not so well ate some toast for supper, which disordered my stomach, & I had another vomiting spell last night.

16th Great excitement in town, the State Troops came in town about 2, o'clock, they had been marshalled at a moments notice, no military preparations, heard the Federalist were near town & determined to meet them, went out & entrenched themselves in the thicket where they were entirely concealed from the Federalist.

17th Every body crazy, there was a battle early to-day. The State troops made a few fires, which was effective wounded 8, I don't know how many were killed; but they were so undisciplined they did not heed an order, & retreated in haste, had they remained & fired the whole Federal army might have been killed. As it was one of the state troops more bold than wise came out into the road & was shot dead, a most excellent citizen. The Federalist advanced to Fulton & took possession, Oh! it makes me boil to see them raise the Flag & huzzah over it. To think I must submit is gaulding, but Fulton is union & most people don't mind their being here. I don't look at them if possible.[24] All wanted me to leave town but I begged off at last, I was not much excited. Mrs. McKinney came in, in the midst of it all. She stood it at first right well, but soon after the Flag was raised she fainted three times before she could be gotten to her bed, she is strong secessionist. Oh! it is so humiliating to me to have them here. Mr. Diggs, Tom & Whiting came after dinner, I was so unwell I did not see them until after supper.

18th Every thing quite still, but I feel worse than on yesterday, not excited, but mad & grieved at our condition; there are not many to sympathize with me. *Most* all feel they are protected; as *they* say most of the State troops were not principled men & were so opposed to Fulton they would not have minded burning the place. What will be the end of this matter whether the Federalist will stay here no one can tell. The state troops are scattered in every direction; there are about 400 Federalist here, the wounded are at Whaley's Hotel, they have taken the C.H. for camp ground. Oh! me how can I stand it?

19th Mrs. Kerr sent me word to write a letter & she would send it to Va which I most gladly did, I have not heard a word from home since I left, Oh! dont I wish I was in Dixie. I felt so secure in Va. Mr. Diggs went home to-day, Mrs. Mc out in the country, Matt in the evening went up to cousin Sue's expecting to see the soldiers come in, none came. Most beautiful night, Mr. C. & my-self went to church with Matt & then went for her, she spent the night at Mr. Lawthers.

20th Mr. C. very unwell it is so hard for him to gain any strength. Staid at home until late in the evening. Matt went to church, Henry Watkins came home with her, had a slight dish of *Secession talk* but I try to keep my tongue as much as possible it does no good to talk. McNeil's Regiment is to drill this evening, Matt is going, the last sight I want to see; she & some one else went in cousin Sue's carriage, walked back with Mr. Marchmore. I feel still very blue about matters. Mrs. McKinney seemed completely over-come. I dont know whether it is this altogether, but she dont have anything to do, not even with Matt, wants to leave town & stay away.

July 21st Commenced raining in the night, was raining at breakfast. About 10 o'clock, we heard a loud blast of music, when a Regiment of Federalist made their appearance. I didnt have the heart to look at them, it was a Col Hammer's company. The most deperate characters, had pillaged the neighborhood through which they passed, & began very early to make depredations here, seeking shelter where they choose & taking what they fancied. It was truly a miserable Sunday it rained too hard for anybody to go to church, & every body was in a state of consternation as to what the troops might do, Oh! I wished 10,000 times to be in Virginia where I felt protected; but here you cant tell what minute a row will happen. The night passed off quietly greatly to our relief & surprise.

22nd The Barbarians left this morning on the road. When they stopped the people prepared provisions for them & thus conciliated them, they were the dread of the country. Nothing unusual today. Mr. McNeils company still here, & deport themselves well. Matt went to cousin Sue's in the evening. Cousin Mary spent the morning here, she has been to Bloomfield a week. I have gotten quite well again.

23rd Henry Watkins, Whiting Diggs, Sam & Matt Lawther & Matt Curd, & self all in my rooms, had a pleasant time. Some soldiers came back, when Henry Halloed hurrah! for Jeff Davis which I repeated; but got quite a lecture for it, at the supper from [several words thoroughly erased] which I drank much fancy but kept my tongue for a some what wonder. The Soldiers of McNeil, made a Federal Flag, hoisted it, & called for three cheers, not one was made except by the Soldiers, which greatly enraged them; but they made no demonstration of violence; they left during the night. Heard to night of a terrible battle at Manassas Junction reports are contradictory about the number of killed & wounded, but the Federalist pronounce it a defeat to them, have not heard the other side at all, there must have been great slaughter from the forces arrayed. Oh! it is awful times. God give us strength to stand it.

July 24th Nothing new about town. Mr. Quarles was here this morning. We had a good talk about Virginia, he is Secessionist & wanted to know all about Southern matters. He, Mrs. Kerr, Mr. Marchmore took tea here. Mr. M tried him self in the talking line, it is such a pity he has so much levity, he ought to be kept in the pulpit is awfully home sick. Mrs. Kerr is to leave the Asylum in a few days, it has broken up, am so sorry they will be a great loss to all.[25]

25th   No body here I dont think, yes there was cousin Mary & Mag Scott spent the morning with me. Matt had Communion Service at her church & was gone some time. Henry Walkins spent the night here, no more reliable news than before about the battle, it is still considered a defeat of the Federalist. Some of the men who had been kept away by the Soldiers, for fear of being arrested as they had been in the fight, came back to-day, & tonight with others went around town serenading with an old hand organ, & singing Dixie. It displeased the Surgeon & wounded soldiers & some say they sent for more troops no body knows whether it is so or not.

26th   Sewed busily all day every thing still so far.

27th   Mrs. Wilson here soon this morning. Matt went down street a little while, very warm day, Matt went to cousin Sue's this evening. I was at home all day.

28th   Weather excessively warm did not go to church.

29th   Very warm. Sewed busily all day. Brother John came to night about 10'clock. I slept up stairs on the porch with Matt. He looks as usual.

31st & 30th   Still hot. Mrs. McKinney has not come back yet.

August 1st   Matt went with cousin Sue to Mr. Marchmore to spend the night. Mrs. Overton came in after tea. Mr. Curd & myself walked home with her. No news about war matters.

August 2nd   Mrs. McKiney came home this morning, her spirits are still very low. More Federal troops arrived this week are camping at the Fair Ground. The Convention has declared Governor & Leut. Governor & Secretary as no longer such & elected one themselves. Judge Gamble of St. Louis is the Governor elect. Various conjectures as to the effect of this move upon the people. They are to be considered as in office until November, when the people decide what is to be done. Missouri is certainly in a distressed condition, none can divine the final issue in these matters.

August 3rd   No rain & still exceedingly hot. I was delighted to get a long letter from home to-night, the first since I left there All were well, they confirmed most statements as regards the Manassas Battle. Great victory to the Confederates. None of our relations were hurt as heard from.

4th   Staid at home all day. Mr. C. & brother John did too, there was no comfortable place to be found.

5th Concluded to go right to work to move. Matt & Mrs. Mc went up this morning to see to the cleaning & worked like heroes, the paint had to be washed. We will have to put up with little troubles; but hope we will get along by degrees, will cook in the cellar at first. *Kitchen* commenced this morning.

6th Up at the house making a carpet, I did not go all said I must not risk it. I hate not to be able to do it. But not my will.

7th The carpets were put down to-day, & put up what curtains we had, we could go right away if the cellar was ready, it is mighty cool & sweet up there.

8th Brother John, Thom & Whiting Diggs went away this morning, shall miss them especially brother J, it is very warm & no rain. Cousin Mary up here a little while this morning. Matt & Mrs. Mc went to Mr. Lawther's. Mrs. Mc heard from Mr. Mc but seems very discouraged, he dont speak of comming till Fall & no suit decided what she will do no body can say.

9th Still excessively warm clouds gather & disperse without rain, up to the house a little while this evening have concluded to build a cold house for the present Kitchen.

10th Busy sewing until evening went up to see to filling the beds & pillows very warm, but had some rain at night.

11th Cloudy & sultry, every body went to church. It cleared off very warm & to night there was a powerful rain & great deal of thunder & lightening, every place leaked it had been so dry. It will make a quantity of corn. Crops of all sorts *fine*.

August 12th I staid at home & sewed. I am well but afraid to do much active work at this time. Mr. Marchmore here a little while last night to say goodbye is going to see his Mother & his eyes dance like a boy the first time he goes home after going to school. He is a curiosity every way.

13th Mrs. Mc & Matt went to church to night. Mr. Ben George led the meeting staid a long time. We have been busy covering boxes for ottomans.

14th Still busy about our boxes, have been *bothered* the reason they werent done sooner. Jenny Nicholson came in this evening here a little while.

15th Moved my room furniture & got it fixed up & Mr. Curd & myself slept up there. Seemed right strange at first; but we will have a mighty comfortable & convenient home. If we only had peace; but things are in such terrible condition I feel encouraged to do any thing scarcely toward permanent plans. Expected aunt

Martha home to night but the St. Aubert hack did not come. News came last night of a terrible battle at Springfield, it lasted all day great number killed both sides. Lyon the Federal General was Killed, of course we cant hear the truth about all things. The Fulton company was in the fight have not heard a name of the killed or wounded. Mrs. Mc in distress about Lute who belongs to this company. Matt, Mrs. Mc, Betty Nicholson, & Mr. Dedmon, came up last night & tried to give us a surprise after we had gotten to the house. I was moving around in my night clothes arranging my ward-robe & bureau, & created quite a stir when they came in. Brother Ed started to St. Louis to get some things for the house & store am afraid he will have trouble on account of military matters. I reckon every thing is terrible in St. Louis. So many idlers & lawless Germans.

16th   Matt at the house. I wrote home to-day, have heard of a new way hope it is reliable as there is no communication by mail between the seceeded & Federal States. We have to send a letter into these states to have it mailed so it will go. I will send this to a man in Kentucky who advertises to send it to Tenesee & have it mailed for any seceded state if you send him 15cts. My letter by Adams Express cost me 28cts it seems like going back-wards, but if I can only hear I can afford to pay as home is the only place to which I write when I used to have most a dozen correspondents. Betsy Nicholson staid all night here, cousin Mary & daughters are in, to meet aunt Martha great disappointment at her not coming. Mr. Curd & myself slept up in the house.

17th   Matt & I went up to the house directly after breakfast, expected to eat dinner there, but couldn't get the stove up. I had mine sent to me. Cousin Mary Nicholson here in the evening & staid to supper. Mr. Lawther's leg is much worse they will send for Dr. Pope of St. Louis, it has been 9 weeks since it was broken. Aunt Mary not come yet.

18th   Staid at home. Matt & Mrs. McKinney both sick. No preaching in town Mr. Marchmore gone home & Mr. Bouland to preach in the country. Betty N. here most all day. Expect Dr. Pope to-morrow. This is our first Sunday at home.

19th   Mrs. Mc went home soon this morning, Matt down town to get some things. I projected about, "fixing things" until dinner time, after that served, Fanny Barbour came up & staid until after supper. Mr. Curd down town so I was left to my meditations. Dr.

Pope came & in five minutes time had performed the necessary operation he didn't think the leg ought to be amputated. Mr. Morton the Irish preacher came to see Mr. Lawther to-night. Aunt Martha not here yet, it seems hard for her to get home. Betty N. came home with Matt about 11, o'clock & we were all relieved to hear of Dr. Pope's decisions.

20th Aunt Martha & Matt Watkins came to-night. Matt went to see her a few minutes. Dr. Pope went home this morning. Made some damson preserves, begin to feel quite settled. Matt went to prayer meeting, Mr. C & myself staid at home.

21st Nothing unusual today.

22nd Jobing about all day. Matt went to prayer meeting & Matt & Henry & Mrs. Watkins with Mr. Dedmon came back with her. To-night is lovely so bright & pleasant. Not had a word from home yet. Oh! it is so hard to be out off from home in this way & things are growing worse.

August 23rd Dont think of any thing of interest.

24th Cousin Mary Nicholson came home this morning & staid until after dinner. Matt quite unwell, cousin M persuaded her to take a dose of oil. I felt badly & had, had pains during the night & day, they grew worse, after dinner I sent for cousin Mary who was up stairs & asked her what she thought of the case, she said I was going to be sick so I made my plans for it, sent for Mrs. McKinney & cousin Mary & later for Dr. Abbott. About supper I was taken with sick stomache, which lasted all night only ceasing while the pains were on me. I was not relieved until half past 5 o'clock in the morning at which hour the baby was born. I had heard all say there was suffering, but the half had not been told.

25th This morning at 5 o'clock, Adele May was born. She is the littlest creature, only weighs 6½lbs., & if likeness can be traced in a baby she is a perfect Curd. At first it was thought she was dead, but she came too sneezing & coughing. Has been sick all day, had something like a spasm which scared us all very much. I was as comfortable as possible to-day.

26th 27th 28th 29th 30th 31st This week, the weather was bright & pleasant some quite warm days. I was in bed, some persons called, but I only listened did not talk as I was afraid of being made sick. The baby has been fretful all week, particularly at night she suffers from stranguary, it is so distressing to see such a little thing suffer, tried all sorts of things but nitre relieved her. Mrs.

McKinney & Matt staid in the room & took care of the baby. They were so kind to me.

September 1st Lovely day, no preaching in town. Mr. Marchmore has gone home for three weeks. This is the second Sunday this has been the case so unusual for Fulton. Mrs. McKinney went home with a sick head-ache.

2nd 3rd 4th 5th 6th 7th Staid all this week in bed, am unusually well, did not have fever when my milk came, the baby is better than she was, but fretful at night. Company came in at different times. News came that Martial law has been declared by Fremont, who has been made Brigadier General, & who assumes kingly authority.[26] One act declares that the negroes of those who are disloyal to the Government shall be declared free. All who go, or come through St. Louis have to take the oath. Things are in the most distracted condition, each party seems to try how it can injure the other party & depradations of all kinds are committed. Mails are almost stopped. There has been a terrible battle fought at Springfield, great loss of life. None of the Fulton company killed. The Captain McIntyre, was very severely wounded, if not fatally. Furniture came this week. I have not seen it. Matt likes it. They moved me into my own bed stead which I like very much. How I wish I could write home.

September 8th Bright & warm. Put on my wrapper & got up this morning felt very weak, sat up only a short time. Matt went to church Mr. Curd staid with me. Mr. Marchmore gotten home.

9th 10th 11th 12th 13th 14th Still keep well lie down most of the time, but feel I am gaining strength; have fine appetite & every thing agrees with me. Nothing unusual either in politics, or domestic matters happened this week. Got a letter from Mr. Stevenson. He had not heard from cousin Angy just a days travel, since last May. Oh! it is so trying. Heard that Mr. & Mrs. Bell were in, from Texas for a short time, wish they could come here.

15th Weather continues delightful, I forgot we had had some disagreeable rainy spell of several days, also that Dr. Young made Matt a visit last week. I of course did not see him. Matt carried the baby in to see him.

16th I am going all about the room, how grateful, I should be for such good health. May I not be unmindful of these blessings. How gratified they should be to hear of it at home.

17th I went into the dining room to dinner, am so glad to be about again. Hate to be dependant so very much.[27] Mrs. McKinney not up to-night. Matt spent the night with her she had the sick head-ache. I forgot to day that a company of Federalist came in Sunday (15) they had not a mouthful to eat; & of course visited very freely the town people only staid until Monday morning, from here they go to Jefferson. Nothing seems to be known of their or the State Troops movements. Uncertain times these.

September 18th Cloudy & sunshine alternate all this week. Mrs. Mc not well enough to come up. The baby keeps well except the colic which she has a good deal; it is hard to get her bowels regulated. Matt put up a few peaches. Henry Watkins here in the afternoon staid until after supper; the baby fretful all evening. Henry became quite disgusted with matrimony in general & babies in particular.

19th Matt went to prayer meeting, Mr. Curd went by for Mrs. McKinney to come up but Rainy had a violent head-ache & she couldn't come.

20th Cloudy & cool, real wintry looking. Matt went to cousin Sue's in the evening heard Rainy was very sick, & went around to see him found him *ill* with congestion of the brain & liver sat up with him all night he was perfectly delirious. Mr. Austin went to St. Louis in company with some others to take care of some patients who were sent home. Quite all have left the Asylum, it is distressing to think of what will become of these lunatics turned loose many of them with out a friend to care for them. Fulton is quite deadened by the effects of this war. both Asylums closed. No College & no Seminary open. horrors!! Am sorry Mr. & Mrs. Kerr, & the managers of the Lunatics Asylum have to leave they will be missed.

21st Matt came home this morning to put up some peaches, Rainy no better. I hope he may get well. Mrs. Jane Barbour came up soon after dinner, then Mrs. Henderson & Miss Matt, everything seemed to be more confused, than I ever saw it. I had been liing down & jumped up in a hurry to take the baby, but it is no use to mind trifles. Mrs. B staid until after supper, Matt went with her down, to spend the night with Mrs. McKinney but came back Mr. B was there. The baby had a hard spell of colic. Mrs. B is looking quite "interesting" it spoils her appearance very much. I am sorry for her. Mr. B has not fixed plans & she feels so unsettled deliver me from a fickle man. His plan on hand at this time is—to go South

& look for a situation as a teacher.[28] He will go on with a party who are going from here to Texas. I wish I was in "Dixie."

September 22nd   Brilliant day. I went out & walked nearly to the fence felt right tired from it. Mr. Robert Dyer came home with Matt from church. It is so sad that he has commenced his bad habits again. I am afraid he is beyond redemption. Matt staid all night with Mrs. McKinney Rainy decidely better. Still another Sabbath at home it has been so long since I have had the privilege of going to church. I hope my time has not been lost.

23rd   Matt started to see the Hockadays soon this morning. Soon after she left Mrs. Price & Miss Lizzie Hockaday came here. She heard they were in town & did not go out. Miss Lizzie came & nursed the baby a little while. She seems so devoted to babies, I wish I had her tact & love for them. Matt went to cousin Sue's, I laid down by the baby to keep her asleep some one knocked at the door, & Mrs. Wilson came in. She sat a short time. Then came Mrs. Hayden to make her first visit. The baby was up so she had to be asked into the chamber; she made many apologies for not calling before; found her very pleasant. While she was here Mrs. Humphreys came & sat until nearly dark. Matt did not come to supper. About 8 o'clock. Joana came up, saying Miss Matt said I must send Mr. Marchmore a suit complete of Mr. Curd's clothes, I was non plused to know what she meant, when she said he & Mr. Tuttle had been out hunting & had gotten covered with Seaticks, & couldn't keep on his clothes. I sent the articles, but he was so long even Mr. Curd's pants were too short; they (the ticks) will give him some fits I reckon.

24th   Mrs. Manchester made a short visit soon after breakfast. Dont know of any thing of importance to-day.

25th   Coming on finely with the kitchen, expect it to be done by the last of October.

26th   Matt went to cousin Sues to dine with Mr. Kerr, the latter here to-night with Mr. Marchmore they had some pretty [unreadable word] talk on hand part of the time but Mr. Kerr was so unwell he was not like he used to be. Matt spent the night with Mrs. McKinney, cousin Sue & Mr. Tuttle here to night.

27th, 28th, 29th, 30th   I don't know anything. Went through the usual routine of nursing.

October "1861" 1st   One days experience is pretty much that of all, forgot to say I went to Mrs. McKinney's & Dr. Abbotts on the

28th spent the day with aunt Ann the first time I had seen her since she had gotten home her health continues about as usual. I am sorry it is so long a walk from here, there could go so conveniently before we moved. The baby is as well as most babies are when so young, she has the colic. She went to see aunt Ann with me. I felt very tired both going & coming. Rainy Mc. much better. Matt went to prayer meeting & from there to Mrs. McKinney's.

2nd 3rd 4th 5th   The same old style, very little of visitors, Matt has been off some where most of the time, I have spent my time nursing. [sentence erased] Dr. Hines brought his piano here the 5th for us to keep didn't know when he should ever call for it. Political Matters as distressing as ever. There has been a battle at Lexington, which resulted most favorably for the State Troops captured a large quantity of money & matter. Oh if we could only see one faint hope of better times.

6th   Intended going to church but the baby had the colic until it was too late, a little baby takes up a great deal of time. To-day is beautiful, after so much rain as has been falling.

7th   Staid in doors closely; baby grows some, made some tomato pikle.

8th   Matt went to Mr. Nicholson's this morning, one of cousin M's sons's cut his knee with a drawer knife & it is doubted if he lives. Cousin Mary The Misses Martin & Matt Walkins here this evening. Joe still here. Henry went to see him thinking he was very sick it was a false report. The sale at the Asylum to-day & yesterday. This is such a breaking up. Fulton is gone now all the public institutions are closed. I am too sleepy to write more so good night!—

9th   No one came in to-day, had a quiet day. Nursing the baby. Mr. Nichol's sale to-day, great many came by here going to it. Things sold well, sale continued at the Asylum. Mr. Curd came up to dinner suffering with the nettle rash, was in bed all the evening, he is most of the time sick, from his cough, nothing benefits him.

October 10th   Rained fast all day. Betty & Jinny Nicholson & Matt came in to the Asylum sale, but it had been discontinued. Matt was not up here. They must have had a hard time, Charly Nicholson some better. Mr. Curd at home all day, I feel so uneasy about him he is so reduced, & his appetite very poor.

11th   Beautiful & mild sent for Aunt Ann to spend the day, she came in the wagon; dear old creature I love to be with her, she seems left here to show what sustaining power there is in Grace. Sent a letter home the other day, got Mr. George to take it to Arkansas to mail. I know they are so anxious about me. Oh! what a trial not to hear from home. I feel perfectly restless about it at times; but try to feel reconciled, by confidening them to God to take care of & watch over them. We are confined to only one side of the picture of affairs out here, I am glad I have the liberty of *thinking* as I please. We get no news except through a Republican medium. Cousin Mary came with aunt Ann, they are *"Union"* then, I have stopped talking, but keep a mighty thinking.

12th Lovely day. I was busy making yellow pickle. Lina staid with the baby while I was out. She is growing some & getting sweeter, & sweeter; how the little nature enlist one affections. Have been up here two months & not been out but twice. Mr. Robinson, Senior, is staying at Mrs. McKinney, & she could not come to see me, I miss her so so much. Nothing new in politics.

13th Bright as possible. I left the baby with Ann & went to the Methodist church large congregation. Mr. Bouland gave a most excellent practical sermon he is truly a godly man. Mr. Marchmore gone to Synod only went out in the morning.

14th Lina took the baby for me to cousin Virginia's this morning she was so good I staid until after dinner, & from there went to see aunt Ann. Mr. Lawther very low spirited about his leg, he has been confined for four months, I hope it may be sanctified to him.

15th Cloudy & damp to-day want to go visiting, but could not for this reason. Cousin Mary here late in the evening, alone the rest of the day, but not lonesome.

October 16th Spend the day with cousin Sue, old Mrs. Robinson there, she is remarkable for her age, 76. Mrs. Allen there also. Synod people have not come. Mr., now Captain, Dunn here yesterday evening said he was going out to see Matt. He must be persevering young man.

Oct. 17th Mrs. McKinney here this morning, cousin Mary came up & we went out calling until after 12, o'clock. I was so much in arrears to my friends in paying visits I had to make short calls made six or seven this morning. All seemed to think I looked better than before the baby was born. Late to-day at the Deaf & Dumb Asylum, both this & the Lunatic Asylum are selling out everything. We may look out for Soldiers being quartered here this winter, so much spare building. I truly hope they may not be.

18th   Went early this morning calling, first to see Mrs. Kerr, who is staying with Mrs. Henderson. She was gone to the Lunatic Asylum sale. I made four or five visits this morning found every body in & doing well. The times are generally discussed, I found Union and Secession in the same family. This question is dividing more families than any other that has ever stirred the public mind. What the end is to be, only the eye of omnicience can say. *Lord* prepare me for every emergency. The most painful thing to me is not hearing from home, not but once since I left there the 17*th* June; & no *hope* of hearing. *"No hope"*. Matt came in today. Mrs. Nicholson's little boy, no better opened Mr. Lawther's leg or rather the box, & found it had knit great relief to all. Mrs. Mc. spent the night here.

19th   Mrs. Robinson, Mrs. Kerr, Miss Matt Henderon & cousin Va Lawther, Mrs. Mc & Mr. Marchmore dined here to-day. Had quite an accident happen to the custard, there was a leak in the freezer & just as it was doing finely discovered that there was more salt coming in than palatable, & the whole thing was spoiled, opened some peaches for substitute. Cousin Lizzie Dyer, Miss Mary Provines called also Mrs. Snell. The baby was unwell all day has a cold & colic. Weather beautiful. The Deaf & Dumb Asylum caught a fire; but it was put out before much injured. Report came a fight was to be out near the [unreadable word], but it did not take place. The Federalist did not come there as expected.

October 20th   Lovely Sabbath. Baby not well early this morning but got to sleep in time for me to go to Pres: church, the second time since I went to Virginia. Mr. Marchmore preached to the children a most suitable sermon, they put to shame the grown people in giving attention & sang very sweetly, regret so much I have to give up my class. School prosperous. Came home the baby had been asleep but she was restless all evening; got to sleep in time for me to go to church Mr. M preached a most excellent sermon to the unconverted. Oh! that Mr. Curd might be made to consider & not harden his heart. He is very unwell his cough seems to grow worse I am very uneasy about him.

21st   Had a chance to send a letter to one of the Seceded States. hope they will get it, want them to hear from me if I cant from them. but I have to be circumscribed for fear it may be broken open & give the carrier trouble I tell you we are living in perilous times. Lewis McKinney came today only to stay a short time. Late in the evening aunt Martha & cousin M, came & I persuaded them to spend the evening. Mrs. Mc. & Mr. Marchmore here too. Had some elegant ice cream. Baby quite sick all day. I am too sleepy to write.

22nd No body here this morning, invited to Dr. Abbott's to take tea with Mrs. Kerr Matt went I could not leave the baby. Mr. Dunn came in the evening Matt wouldnt see him, I dont know *why*. I went to prayer meeting the second time since March a good lecture, but Oh! how few were out, men's minds cant rest on any subject but the *War*. Church quite cold, Mr. Curd coughed. I am so uneasy about his cough. Oh! that he might be led to consider his latter end.

23rd Mrs. McKinney up here soon this morning, Matt went to cousin Sue's to sew on the machine for her. I went to Dr. Abbott's left the baby there & went over to cousin Sam Dyer's, cousin Lizzie laughing as usual. Spent the day at Dr. Abbott's. Brother John came this evening. Mr. Dedmon came after tea & when he left Matt went to Mrs. Mc. as usual. There is a camp of State Troops about 12 miles from here. Report says Federal Troops are coming to attack them. I hope we may be spared a battle near us. Dont hear any thing from the south but through the Republican. Bad chance this.

October 24th Mr. Dunn here to day from 10 o'clock until after four, considerable sitting this. Had quite an amusing time at dinner. There was the toughest kind of chicken so much so that every body nearly, left the original piece on his or her plate; & the cream was so poor, that I felt the credit of the family was below par for palateable dinners. Not a line from home Oh! how I long to hear from them. I sit & conjecture,—my only resource. Today the partnership of Curd & Bro- was dissolved Mr. John Curd selling his portion to Mr. Edwin. Am afraid Bro John is in a rather bad fix for security ship.

25th Mrs. Mc. here to dinner, had some good fried chicken with the best kind of salsify, most equal to oysters. Mr. Russel here in the morning & evening; he had to leave home on account of his Secession opinion, says we cant form an idea of the condition of things in the upper country on the other side of the river, depredations of all kinds committed & a number of his neighbors taken prisoners, terrible times truly. Mr. Bouland here this afternoon, he is purely good as ever. Oh! What a crown he will in the day of reckoning. Intended going to Jude Hockaday; but they kept us from it. About dark Matt & Henry came over the latter staid to tea. Brother John went home with her. Mr. Curd gone down town & Matt as usual at Mrs. Mc. [long erasure]²⁹ Couldn't go to Judge Hockaday, as these came in.

26th   Most beautiful & balmy day like Spring. Matt & I went to see the Miss Hockaday they insisted on our staying all day, & said they would not call it a visit until we did come so. Every thing was so still & quiet I told Matt it looked as if they were beyond the hearing of War news. The old Judge was generally complaining & "not so well after all." We came home & Matt went to cousin Va in the evening so I was alone. The baby is as fat as a butter ball, is getting so interesting. No War news.

October 27th   Pretty day. Went to church very small congregation. Mr. Marchmore complained of not feeling well but his services were very long. Dr. Scott had his baby baptized. Went to church at night; very solemn sermon.

28th   To-day about 800 Federal troops arrived on a keen lookout for Secessionist, those who had taken up arms fled in a hurry. The officers forbid the guard let man woman or child pass without "*a pass*" isnt this outrageous? I trust a better time is coming.³⁰ Invited to cousin Va to dinner went Mr. L. seems in fine spirits having the federals here Oh! he is so strong, that is a divided family on this subject. What a seperation this question is, - *Secession*, or *Union*. I kept perfectly silent this is my only chance for if once started I become excited and can do no good.

29th   Matt went with Mrs. Mc. to cousin Sue's to make a pair of jeans pants; they came to dinner and left directly after. Mr. Dunn here twice to see if Matt was at home, he must keep up a good heart to hold on so to the end. Went to prayer meeting. The baby is so good she doesn't get up until late in the morning. Not a sylable from home yet it is great trial so to be.

30th   Things go along in the same old routine.

31st   Miss Marie Beckenbaugh married this morning to a Mr. Young. Will Austin went & bro Ed was invited. In the evening cousin Mary Abbott, Miss Matt Henderson & Mrs. Overton were here, the latter, to get subscriptions for getting a carpet for the church, said Mrs. Allen gave them a blessing for wanting to fix up Mr. Marchmore. Cousin M staid to tea & until bed time. Matt went to church & Mr. Curd with her, so were left to our selves until 8 o'clock, when bro John came from Mr. Lawther's. A most outrageous letter in that most outrageous sheet, the Democrat advising government, to send troops here to winter in the Asylum. He ought to be hung nearly. Mr. & Mrs. Robert Dyer here to dinner.

November 1st Today is cloudy & gloomy looks like we might have snow, kitchen finished, not dry enough to go in it. No news of any kind. Matt & bro John gone to cousin Sue's to supper. Mr. Curd down town so I am still alone, but I [half line erased] but Mr. C. stays but a short time down town. I get so sleepy these nights I am shamed of myself. Baby keeps well & grows fast.

2nd Brother John took dinner with Mr. Junius Robertson. All came very late to dinner. Matt went to Mr. Lawther directly after dinner. Mr. Dunn started up here, saw her going away & turned back. Henderson's company came this evening, it makes me sick at heart to think of any more Federals being here; but I will try & guard my mouth lest I sin with my tongue. These are times when Christians should be very careful how they act; but Oh! cold & stupid the church seems to every thing but politics, how can we expect a blessing!!

3rd To day is lovely & mild went to church. there were a plenty of Federal's out, there are between 7 & 800 men. Great many old people out Mr. M. must have anticipated it, as he preached to the aged. Cousin Martha & Mr. Dunn here to tea. Brother John went with cousin M to church. Mr. D ventured with Matt, I wouldn't risk the chance of being taken up, he has been a Capt. & they are glad to get any of what *they* call "rebels". Mr. D found they were in search of him & went to Mrs. McKinney. Staid there all night & until after dinner without seeing any one so if they came she might say she hadn't seen him.

4th Weather still pretty. Mr. D sent for his horse but it was missing. Matt went to Mrs. Mc. soon after dinner. Preaching in the Methodist church to night to continue during the week. Matt went, I staid with Mr. C., & brother John.

5th Rather cloudy. Cousin Virginia here to breakfast. Brother John started home soon this morning. I shall miss him. Every thing very quiet, the soldiers behave very well so far. I couldnt go to prayer meeting to night, baby was not well.

6th Carried the baby to see aunt Ann. Went by Mrs. Mc. She was going to the Methodist prayer meeting, ran over to the Pres:

church to see what they were doing lots of women there scrouring & scrubbing the benches. They got such sights had to have their dinner sent. We sent Letitia Henderson some said all her fault was that there was not enough. I went to Mrs. Grant & cousin Sue's in the evening.

November 7th   Cousin Sue took me & aunt Martha out to Mr. Snell's, spent a very pleasant day, the baby was not well but very good. the ride was very pleasant. roads like in the Summer. got back about dark; Matt had gone to Mr. Lawther.

8th   Went to prayer meeting this morning, very few out. Mrs. Mc. here a little while came to see if she could find a piece of carpet for our seat at church. Went to church at night.

9th   Lovely day & very mild. Jinny Nicholson spent the day here. In the evening there was a might *ado* about raising the flag, speech by Henderson, two cannon fired &ᶜ. I had no desire to be there. Matt Jinny N. Mrs. Abbott & Lawther went out to their camp it was too much for Jinny & she had to take a cry & gave some short talk to the officers.

10th   Rather cloudy early, but bright the latter part of the day. Mr. Curd very unwell did not go out. I went to the Methodist church house full; had communion service. Mr. Robinson the presiding elder preached an hour & 5 minutes. did not go out at night Mr. C so complaining.

From this time to December 20th   I neglected to write regularly & must give an abridged account of what happened as I remember. Mr. Curd continued to grow worse until I got Matt to write to Dr. Young of Columbia, as he did not seem willing to have any of these Drs. practice on him; he came quite soon examined Mr. Curd, pronounced he had bronchitis, staid only a day, came near being killed going back, the horse ran away with the buggy. He sent the medicine down which with blistering helped Mr. C very much. Oh! I am so anxious about him, if he were prepared great God open his eyes to see his condition. Cousin Laura has been up to see aunt Ann, who has been very ill, she has much improved. Matt has been to Mr. Kerr & spent a week, Miss Tish Henderson went with her had a nice time. Mr. Marchmore went out to assist Mr. Morton to preach in Mexico, very interesting meeting. Mrs. Kerr came home with Matt staid two days. Had the baby baptized the 1st Sunday in December, she behaved beautifully named her *Martha Hart* as the men were so opposed to fancy names. She is growing fast but has the colic badly. No war news of importance all seem as determined to fight as ever. Not a word from home & no hope of any thing. Oh! it is a sore trial not to hear from my dear family I feel some times that I cant stand it. Missouri is in a most horrible condition, a kingly government would be preferable no news from the South except what comes by the Federal papers, so many falsehoods are told I dont care to read the papers. I am *more & more Southern.*

December 15th   Weather most beautiful & has been for some time more like Spring than Winter. Went to church Mr. Marchmore preached to the children. Gave a most solemn sermon. Take heed *how* you hear, take heed *what* you hear. Mr. C. stays mostly in the house. The Methodist began a meeting today.

16th   Bright as possible. Went down to see aunt Ann in the evening & from there rode out to Mr. Robert Dyer's. Mrs. D looks as if she was lowered down with trouble. Mr. D is drinking again poor man I am afraid he will be given up this time.[31]

17th   Still very lovely weather could not go to prayer meeting because the baby had the colic. She has it worse than when she was first born.

18th   Nothing new under the sun. Went to prayer meeting this morning not many out sent the baby to see cousin Sue; Mr. C. not well.

19th   Had the lard of two hogs to dry up. Miss Lizzie Hockaday came home with Matt, & during the evening Mrs. & Miss Martin, & Mr. Bouland came.

20th   Nothing of interest today in [long erasure] for more Grace.

21st   Went to the Methodist church to preaching, came home found Mr. Edwin Curd has been up, report was abroad that State Troops were coming to Fulton, the "Union" people were all agog on the subject, but the Federals came up every thing was right. I never said a word. My great aim is to keep perfectly silent I pray constantly to be able to keep a guard on my tongue. Things getting worse instead of better.

December 22nd   Snowed hard this morning, did not go to church. Mrs. McKinney came up after preaching. Matt went to cousin Sue's according to custom, as she is there *very very* often. Did not go to church night nor day.

23rd   Weather bright, but some what cold, made some calves feet jelly Matt went to prayer meeting at the Methodist church &

from there to cousin Sues. Mr & Mrs. Mc. came up here after night, & I went with them to the Methodist church to preaching, but a handful of people. Mr. Bouland said it seems useless to continue the meeting. Oh! it is so sad his righteous soul is so vexed. The churches are in a most distressing condition, the war question seems to command the whole attention.

24th   Weather bright & mild a most remarkable winter. The Troops so far have not suffered from the weather. There is a large number of soldiers here from Iowa, have not seen them. I stay at home closely Mr. C. is in doors most of the time, am happy to say he is better, but still feeble, not able the attend to business.

25th   Xmas day I can scarcely believe it to be so, it seems such a short time since the last, although I have gone through many changes & times have been so troubled oh! what a year!—Matt sent for Mr. Tuttle & cousin Sue to breakfast, made some egg-nog & everybody seemed quite merry considering all things. Matt & cousin S. made some ribbon cake. Mr. Curd drank some egg-nog which made him sick. Miss Tish Henderson & Miss Overton came up in the morning. Matt & they had a snow balling. Cousin Virginia sent for us to go down & see the Xmas tree Matt & I went it pleased the children very much. Mr. Thompson Henry Watkins beau came to-day. Weather mild & beautiful a most wonderful Season.

26th   Things happened as usual. At home all day.

27th   Nobody came in to-day but Mrs. McKinney, she came after night to stay with Mr. Curd I went to cousin Sue's didnt feel like it, but thought it best to do so. I have felt so depressed lately, times seem to be darkening instead of brightening. What will the worse be. The Troops here are arresting every body they suspicion at all, from far, and near. The rail Road has been torn up 35 miles below & 35 miles above Mexico & they are trying every body for it & have ordered all who can be proved engaged in tearing up the road shall be shot. Was there ever seen such times? The Federals will have times to keep down what they call the "rebellion." My whole sympathy is for the South. It distresses me so much to think I cant hear from there. But I only confide in my Heavenly father, Who doeth all things well, & can make me feel it to be so.

28th   Mr. Curd did not go out to-day very unwell had a blister drawn, on his throat, the best one he has had yet. Matt & several girls expected to go out to Mr. Snell's by invitation, but report

came there was a battle expected near Williamsburg, & they
thought best not to go, but there was no truth in the report. The
Feds went out, but came back, brought some prisoners, which I am
afraid will get harsh dealing. Mr. John Provines & Capt. McIntire
were taken, they were told on. Capt. M has not recovered from the
wound he got at Springfield, will suffer much. Mrs. Abbott, Watkins, Tuttle & aunt Martha spent the evening here, but my heart
was so heavy it was hard to keep up at all. Mrs. W very uneasy for
fear Joe will be taken. The baby grows weighs 14lb & is mighty
sweet.

 29th   A most beautiful day could not go to church morning, nor
night. Mr. C more unwell than usual to-day.

 30th   Lovely day I went to see aunt Ann a little while in the
evening, first time I have been there for two weeks or no where
else.

 31st   The last day of 1861 Oh! sad to think of times past. Never
in the annals of American History did such a Xmas dawn upon us.
The whole nation in an uproar & turmoil brother seeking brother's blood. I have felt such gloomy foreboding to-day made worse I
suppose by hearing that Mr. Dunn & Mr. Karns had been arrested
& as they had books with by laws & oaths of a society for the cause
of secession I suppose they will be hung or shot. Theirs was a haz-
ardous undertaking & as it has proven most dangerous it seems as
fatality hung over every thing connected with Mrs. McKinney; it
makes my heart sick to think of it. Am writing this at night, it has
just struck seven soon the last sands of 61, will be spent. Help us to
examine ourselves for the past year & by the Grace of God resolve
to live nearer him in the future; so let come what troubles or dark
days may, give me the light of thy countenance & all shall be right.
Fare well 1861. May the sins of this year not be remembered
against me or mine.

 January 1st 1862.   When I remember each event as it happened
in regular order it seems so short a time since 61 came in; But
when I think I think with what big events this year has been
fraught, & how many scenes I have passed through, what a great
change in my situation, feelings &^{c} [etc.] as well as in the Nation it
seems as if ages had rolled by since we welcomed 61. Oh! that 62
might not be in many respects as 61, but that the troubles then
begun may end speedily this year. May the time past in my life be
sufficient for me to lived so far from God & may I & mine be
brought humbly to the foot of the cross & find peace in believing.

Today is hiring day. Mr. C went down this morning to see about some one, took aim again, did not get Ralfe. Every thing looks gloomy at the least to me, for my heart wanders away to my dear home & wonders what they are doing there & if there is a family unbroken four long months have elapsed since I heard from there & what changes may have been wrought. But for the Grace of God I feel, that with Mr. Curd's sickness, my absence, & not hearing from home, & the present troubles of the country, I would sink. Still I have many things to be grateful for & may I not murmur.

2nd   Mr. Curd very unwell to-day, more so than he has been for some time, coughs very much & cant sleep at all. I am so uneasy about him, would that he had a hope for the future. Staid in doors closely go out very very seldom in the first place havent the inclination & I nurse the baby & dont want to leave Mr. Curd. So at home I am found most of the time.

3rd.   Mr. C. still very feeble & coughing did not get up until 12 o'clock. Cousin Virginia came & staid until after dinner (we have only two meals a day). Matt went to Mrs. Mc. as usual. The baby well & growing quite fast.

4th.   Weather has been sleety & very gloomy. My heart has felt much burdened the last week. Am so anxious about Mr. Curd.

5th.   Ground covered with snow & still snowing rapidly did not go to church. Have not been for three Sabbaths. Read as much as I could with nursing the baby.

6th.   Mr. C. is better than he has been for some days. I had a good night's rest. Went down this evening. Matt went with cousin Sue in the wagon & Mr. Marchmore drove, out to Mr. Snell's; who is very sick. I went to prayer meeting this the week of prayer for the world. I thought so much of being so far from those I hold so dear.

January 7th. 62   Weather wintry snow not melting. Mr. C very unwell coughing a great deal. Betty Nicholson came this morning soon after breakfast. Matt went to see Mrs. Kerr, at Mr. Lawther's, the former came back with her & sat a little while. Henry & Matt Watkins here to dinner. I staid most all day in here with Mr. C. I have no heart for company when he is so unwell. Mrs. Mc here also to dinner. All left for church except myself. Mr. C. & I sitting down or he is lying down; the baby in the crib quite restless I am rocking her while writing. If all around us was as quiet as we, three are now, what a blessed state it would be!

8th. to 17th.   Since Mr. Curd has been so unwell, it seems almost impossible for me to do any thing, not, that I wait on him so much, but I just feel anxious & restless so I have not written since the 8th. will try & do better in the future. Nothing of interest has transpired I have been closely at home, not been to church for 4 Sunday. We have had quite heavy snows, & some extremely cold weather. Bro. Ed was at the creek all day Wednesday (15th.) seeing to getting ice we have gotten the house full of beautiful ice. War matters about the same arrests are common & much *pressing* done *from* the Secessionists. The Troops from Iowa still here & likely to remain. I don't see any thing of them unless I go to church. These are trying times. I trust I can keep my tongue. Several nights ago we were awakened by terrible rapping on the front door & then some body hallooed the man said he must see Mr. Curd, who had one of the worse nights *sweats* I ever saw. I told him Mr. C. could not get up, & asked if he wanted to come in said yes, then told him to walk around to the back door, threw my shawl over me & walked to the door & told him to come in, he went right to the bed & said he had been ordered to search every house for fire arms, & wanted to know if there were any here. Mr. C told him no, he remarked as he had heard was a [erasure] man he would take his word. It was all false as to his being ordered, & why he came no human can tell. There has been a case of small pox & [unreadable] among them, am afraid it will extend over town.

January 18th.   Unpleasant misty weather. Miss Tish Henderson here staid all night. Cousin Martha here a little while she seems very sad is uneasy about Joe for fear the Federals will take him Oh! these are gloomy days. I feel to day as if my heart would burst. Mr. Curd is better to-day; but I feel that it is but a short time. To night I had a talk with him upon the subject of religion it was gratifying the way he talked God grant peace to his soul & Grace for him in this his affliction. Oh what dark hours.

19th.   Still cloudy & disagreeable the Sun has shown out but a short time this year; it seems omnious of what this year must bring to all dark days of affliction & trouble in various forms. Mr. C very unwell had quite a hard chill this morning which prostrated him. Staid at home all day, this is the fifth Sunday since I went to church, dont leave Mr. C at all. Brought in Joe Watkins with several other prisoners this evening; am so sorry for his mother. It is hard to see strangers come in & bear rule over us in this way. I try to keep my tongue still but it is a great struggle my heart is with

the South, & [line heavily inked out] Oh! it makes me pant to be in
Dixie where all think alike. No news nor hope of any from home,
how could I be cheerful when thus situated. Mr. Marchmore gone
to St. Louis. Mr. Finley preached for him to-day & night Mrs. Mc
has her head ache.

20th. Things progressing as usual arrests common & the
property of Secessionist daily taken to support the Soldiers here
stationed, wagons loaded pass here with corn thus taken.

21st. Mr. Curd about the same, coughs a great deal at night
sometimes does not lie down until 2, & 3, o'clock at night.

22nd. Cloudy, sleety weather, gloomy without & within.

23rd. Aunt Martha & cousin Sue here to dinner, Mrs. McKinney, cousin Virginia & Martha here in the evening. I have felt unwell all day have the weed in my breast Baby grows fast. Matt &
cousin M went to prayer meeting, the latter is much troubled
about Joe being prisoner.

24th. Rather brighter this morning in fact the sun is shining.
Mr. C had a bad night, but slept until late this morning. Cousin
Thom Dyer came to see him, he has come for cousin Sam Dyer's
children, cousin Lizzie went to St. Louis to see cousin Sam &
begged him into letting her go, they expect to leave for N. Y. Monday. Matt with Henry & Matt Watkins to the asylum to see Mr.
Lakeland who is a prisoner.

January 25th. Bright day, the first day in which the Sun has
shone all day this year. Mr. C went down town in Mr. Lawther's
buggy, (he has been so kind to Mr. C) the second time this year,
enjoyed it very much & had no bad effect, Oh! it makes me so sad
to think of his condition. Made some green pickle. Matt went to
Mrs. McKinney to stay the night.

26th. Cloudy, gloomy weather, Matt staid with Mr. Curd & I
went to church, the first time in six weeks. Mr. Finly preached his
voice is disagreeable, but the subject very good. When I came home
found Mr. C very feeble, slept a long while in the evening. Mr.
VanDoren & Wilson came here, but he was so unwell did not wake
him to see them. Mrs. Mc here.

27th. Sleety & gloomy as possible. Mr. C very unwell weather
unfavorable to him. Nothing new heard from Dr. Young, he had
been arrested by the Federals, was the reason he had not been
down, no body seems safe now, always am anxious for him to see
Mr. Curd. Baby is sweet as possible.

28th.   Raining all day the yard is like a morter bed, have never had it leveled. Mr. C very feeble poor me! [This last comment written in different ink, probably much later.]

29th.   Matt went to cousin Sue's to do some machine work on brother John's shirts, in the evening cousin Mary Abbott came, later Dr. Abbott & then Henry & Matt Watkins. Had quite a pleasant chat. Mr. C much better to-day, but there is no idea how he may be to-morrow.

30th.   Am feeling very much depressed. Mr. C had night sweats last night & is very feeble to-day. Oh! I feel as if my heart would sink within me, when I see him look so badly. I am afraid he is prey to consumption. God in mercy spare him, & make him one of thine own. No tidings from home this makes me unhappy; heard that Mrs. Price was dead, & the moment I wondered how is father. Oh! What dark days trouble on every hand. God help me! Mrs. McKinney here to-day. Matt went to see Mrs. Vaughter poor woman she is in great affliction with her cancer.

31st   Concluded it was best to have a physician at home for Mr. C. Abbott called in made every change it was possible in the practice of Dr. Young, examined Mr. C.'s lungs & pronounced one effected, oh!³² I fear he will never be well again. May he be prepared for whatever change may happen, and me for bearing it.

February 1st.   Mr. C. feeling quite well, went with him to cousin Virginia's the day bright but very muddy.

2nd.   Went to church & Matt staid with Mr. Curd it clouded up & snowed fast in the evening aunt Martha came home with me, Mrs. McKinney here, cousin Sue Will Lawther, & Mr. Junius Robertson came during the evening it did not seem like Sunday, I had no time to read or reflect, Mr. C. had another chill to-day very feeble, commenced quinine in earnest.

3rd.   Mr. C. had another chill very poorly Oh! what a grievous affliction to see one thus stricken down.

4th.   Mr. C. had two chills to-day very prostrate,, heard of Major Snell's illness suppose he will not recover.

5th.   Mrs. Hockaday sent Mr. C. some tripe it seemed to tempt an appetite, his friends have been so kind to him. Walking dreadful, like [unreadable word] the streets.

6th.   No change with Mr. C. another chill to-day heard Major Snell was diing Oh! the amount of trouble in the land, but people will marry nevertheless. Miss Grant & Mr. Cowen were married to-day expected quite a wedding but with sickness & death among the neighbors there were very few; dreadful times to marry.

7th.   Major Snell died last night 71 years old, very much discouraged about Mr. C. chills continue

8th.   Weather bright, Major Snell's funeral to-day was buried with Military Honors (the Federals being here). Mrs. Mc staid with Mr. C. & I went to see aunt Ann found her extremely feeble with a constant cough. Miss Tish Henderson came up & went to the funeral with Matt.

9th.   Did not go to church to-day. Matt & Watkins & Ginny Nicholson here in the evening it seems hard to have a quiet Sabbath. Much amused with the "Nigger" Bruk Read came to see Mr. C., he is half idiot. Matt Watkins told Mr. Curd, she heard Mr. Austin was to be married, & such a teasing as Matt gave him he was confused he couldn't talk.

10th.   Nothing of interest to-day every day seems fraught with intense care for Mr. C. gets no better.

11th.   Prayer meeting evening but I scarcely ever go dont leave Mr. C for any thing. Very muddy about 300 troops passed here to day. I never expected to see that many Federals.

February 12th.   Warm to-day, Mr. C. almost prostrate. I dread seeing the warm weather am afraid he will sink under it. Have had some satisfactory talks with him on the subject of religion & while his evidence is not as bright as I would hope yet I believe him to be a changed man. I pray God he will give him brighter manifestations. Such patience I have rarely witnessed. Oh! my heart feels like it will burst God help me!—Miss Kitty Diggs, Ike, Tommy & Whitening came this evening roads so bad like as not to have gotten here came to see Mr. Curd.

13th.   Gloomy day, suits my feelings. I feel like my strength would give away. Mr. Carr came up to [unreadable word] & staid all night looks so well & eats what he wants. Meeting began to night preparatory to communion. All went from here but myself & Mr. Carr. I hope they may have a good meeting. Turned *very cold*.

14th.   Regular reception day, Cousin Mary & Virginia spent the day. cousin Sue & aunt Martha & cousin Mary Abbott. Mr. C. had another chill, & vomits regularly with them. aunt M brought Mr. C a watch Mr. Edwin Dyer left to Mr. C Mr. Carr & Mr. Marchmore here to-night. All sitting around the fire talking, when Will Austen came in almost breathless, asking if we had heard of the terrible news—Dr. Overton had shot Sam Williams, & Williams shot Overton. it produced a terrible sensation. Mr. Marchmore left to go to the scene of trouble. These are perilous time, but men will not be warned.

15th.   Pretty day but very muddy. Preaching at 11 o'clock. I did not go, had a very solemn meeting I heard. Dr. Overton not expected to live, perfectly conscious & composed, said he shot in self defense. Williams very ill. Mr. Curd very feeble, had a chilll this evening. I feel very much depressed to-day. No news from home. Mr. C's bad health, besides the late defeat of the Confederates & surrender of Ft. Henry are enough for making me sad besides the low condition of the church for it seems as if religion, in the very time it is most needed languishes most. Mr. Marchmore is troubled about his church, says there is much bad feeling among the members. I can say Religion has been most precious in its consolations to me, in my late troubles but for that I feel I must have sunk. Preaching to-night at church.

February 16th.   Matt staid with Mr. Curd & let me go to church. There was Communion service, very few out, but the meeting was most solemn. News came before the service was taken that Dr. Overton was dead, died a most triumphant death. But oh! how melancholly the cause. Mrs. O. seems entirely overcome this is her first trouble, poor woman it came like a thunderbolt. Oh! the anguish which this has caused. Mr. Finly preached an admirable sermon from the text "Christ All in All" full of consolation for these times. Mr. Marchmore came home with me, had prayers with Mr. Curd. Cousin Mary Abbott & Mrs. McKinney here in the evening also Kate Coffman who seems to bear the loss of her little girl with great composure. Will Tucker & Mr. Stuart & Mr. Wilson here this evening to see Mr. Curd. I dont like so many Sunday cant improve the day.

17th.   Miss Kitty & the boys started home today, will miss them. Dr. Overton's funeral preached, large number out I heard. Was disappointed Mr. C could not go. He was buried with Military honors, there being a *plenty* of Feds here.

18th.   Bright morning, prayer meeting at the church at 11 o'clock. Mr. Curd walked down town and staid a short time seemed none the worse for going. He had a dreadful night last night coughed until two o'clock & had a chill which lasted over 2 hours. Henry has been expecting since the middle of the day [unreadable word] Kitty sent for Dr. Abbott to night. She has had a hard time. Went to church to night, very good congregation, nothing of especial interest. Kate Coffman came home with me. Cousin Martha & Mary here to-day; the former is forbidden to see Joe.

19th.   Henry still grunting, but was delivered about 1, o'clock of a man child named Thomas for Mr. C.[33] the latter is about the same has a chill every day which keeps him so weak oh! troubles do not come singly to me, away from home with no tidings of friends, & Mr. C sick it makes my heart sick.

20th.   Preaching to-night a good congregation, but Mr. Marchmore so discouraged that none went up to be prayed for; he broke up the meeting to every body (I heard spoke of it,) sorrow. He promised to come up here & spend the night. I waited for him, but he was sitting on the pulpit sofa his face buried in his hands very sorrowful; but afterwards he came, heard Mr. C coughing & would not come in. Mr. C had a feeble night. I am afraid he will never be well.

February 21st.   Mr. C tolerably well, cousin Sue up here this morning staid until late. Female prayer meeting was there yesterday. The Union people are gone to decorate the College for speaking on to-morrow Matt went this morning. I was not asked as a matter of course. Met one evening at Mr. Hendersons & make arrangements for it. The Feds carry the day here; oh how I long to be in the South; there all are of one mind, whatever the Federal Papers say to the contrary; but here Secesh has to keep its mouth shut, or away to prison. There has been mighty firing of guns as salute to the taking of Fort Donnelson. It grieves me whenever the Confederates are routed. But I am so troubled about Mr. Curd, that Politics are of minor importance. Prayer meeting here no man but Mr. Marchmore, cousin Martha prayed. Mr. C. very feeble could not go in.

22nd.   Guns firing by day; the Feds are out on parade & cutting up generally. Speeches by several at the College. Badges of red, white & blue, given to the Union men of the country. Things generally gay among the town & soldier Feds.

23rd.   [3 lines erased] at night, good congregtion. So many Feds it was suffocating almost. Mr. C tolerably comfortable. Mr. Dyer & Henderson, Dr. & Mrs. Scott came to see Mr. Curd.

24th.   Bright pleasant day. Mr. C. had a chill but rode out afterwards, & walked from down town seemed quite well. Oh! how flattering his disease changes in a few minutes I could be blind to his condition how gloomy I feel. Oh! for grace to sustain me. The baby is as sweet as babies get to be. So like her papa.

25th.   Mr. Curd not so well. Mrs. Henderson & Miss Matt here, & Mr. Marchmore to dinner. Prayer meeting to night. Mr. Wells brought Mr. C. two partriges, & went with Matt to church, if she dont mind Mrs. Wells will get jealous of the old beaux attention. The baby six months old & weighed 16 lbs. is as sweet as children get to be.

26th.   Mr. C. went to ride this morning; but it turned too cold while out, was no better for the ride. Mrs. Snell came just as he started, & spent the day with us, cousin Va., aunt Martha & Mrs. McKinney dined here, Mrs. Henderson & Bailey here in the evening. It is generally a rush or none at all. But my heart is so heavy I feel that every one passes their time in a dull manner. Mr. C very feeble this evening; it is distressing to see a man thus stricken by disease. I trust he has a hope, an enduring one & if God should thus afflict me by taking him, I feel he will be prepared, I pray he may have brighter manifestations of his love & forgiveness. Oh! God may he be spared for great usefulness. Cousin Mary Abbott had company to night. [line erased] I was invited but have no inclination to go into company. [line erased]

27th.   Today is prayer for Colleges over the whole land. Services at the Presbyterian church morning & night, Matt went. Miss Tish Henderson came home with her to dinner, & staid until church at night. Mr. Curd had a chill which lasted him more than 7 hours, he was very weak afterwards, with hard sweats. Oh! I am afraid he will not last long. What dark hours to me but for the Grace of God I would be in perfect despair. How I long to be with father & my family; but many are worse off than I am. Mr. C went to bed early & so did I. When Matt & Mrs. McKinney came home they brought Mr. Bouland with them & I was in bed. I lose so much sleep I thought I would take my chance for a good night's rest. We slept until 4, o'clock when he awoke with a cough, which always precedes, & follows his chill with vomiting, the chill came, & lasted 3 hours. Tis so hard to see him suffering & can give him no relief. Mr. & Mrs. R. Dyer here.

28th.   Nobody in to-day. Mr. C tolerably well in the morning not so in the evening & had a second chill to-day. But he bears it all with the greatest patience & fortitude. Quarterly meeting begins to-night. Matt went to see aunt Ann & from there to church. Windy & cold borrowing from March the last day of winter it seems as a dream, I am sitting by Mr. Curd around the fire he is coughing badly, I am writing but he occupies my thoughts. I wonder where & how all are at home. I shall have to wait a season (I am afraid) before that question is answered. Mr. C had another chill which makes two since 4, o'clock. it seems beyond remedy. Got in a full supply of chickens today a feast or a fast. The baby has a bad cold it distresses to hear her cough am afraid something will happen of it. I trust not to cling too much to her, for we are not permitted to make to ourselves idols & keep them.[34]

March 1st. Had tooth ache last night; this morning got Mrs. McKinney to go down with me soon to Dr. Brewers to have my teeth fixed, he would not pull it, but will fix it. Very gloomy day had a thunder storm last night and hail. This is the first time I have been out since the Feds were here, Oh! what a sight they are & everything so dirty from them. Matt grunting Mr. C had a chill while I was away. Tried taking Cod Liver oil; but his stomach rejects it, poor fellow, I trust his Grace may be as his day. The baby poorly with a cold.

2nd. A Gloomy looking morning. Matt went to church expecting communion, but Mr. Ford forgot to get the wine & it was postponed until night; she said it was unusually solemn at night, the first time I ever knew of its being at night. Elders prayer meeting here this evening, no ladies came I enjoyed it very much; Mr. C was in the room; he has not been well enough for some time to go to church. He had a chill today; but took a long nap after it which refeshed him. Mr. Dedmon brought him some oysters which *he* cooked for him. The baby looked and behaved as sweet as possible, she coughs right much.

3rd. Went soon this morning to Dr. Brewer's; dentist always keeps you going for a season very cold & windy. Mr. Wells brought Mr. Curd a Prairie chicken, he has been so kind to him since his sickness. Jinny Nicholson & Matt Watkins & cousin Mary Abbott here to dinner, cousin Virginia came late in the evening. She expects to go to St. Louis with Mr. Lawther, who is uneasy about his leg, I am afraid he will have more trouble with it. Mr. C had a chill & vomiting spell which lasted over four hours he was more comfortable until this came on.

4th. To-day a year ago Lincoln was inaugurated, a time none will forget for with him begins an era of unprecedented trouble to this Nation. It has been windy & cold, no one here except cousin Sue; Mr. C had another chill but was near so sick from it, a comfortable day altogether. The baby has been as sweet as ever. Matt went to prayer meeting; but to cousin Sue's first to do some [unreadable word]. Commenced smoking the meat to-day. Mr. James Patton & sisters & Miss Matt Henderson & Mr. Tucker started yesterday to Audrain; to Mr. Pattons wedding. The driver got drunk & Mr. Patton had to drive.

March 5th. To day a year ago I started to Virginia Oh! the changes since then, I have been entirely issolated from my dear home, a sore trial it has been; but I trust this with my other troubles have been blest. My heart is sore pained when I see the change wrought in Mr. Curd; it is sad to see the strong man brought low. A very unpleasant day alternate clouds wind & snow—such is life. Mr. C about as usual, I can see no marked change in his disease.

6th. Went this morning to Dr. Brewer's he was not there, & I had to stay over two hours; my tooth aching all the time he could do nothing with my teeth they were so inflamed; I came home & suffered violently all day. It has been a dreadful day snowing & blowing & turning dark & then light. Cousin Martha here this evening. I had a disagreeable night.

7th. Every body feeling badly to-day, Mr. C more unwell than I have seen him for some time great debility. Cousin Va. here this evening. Matt went to a Concert for the benefit of the Sunday school. I forgot to say she went to Mr. Pattons to a party last night, given to the bridal party; she had a very pleasant time & thought Mrs. P. quite a nice lady. There was $30.00 made at the Concert; the male singing was done mostly by the Feds. Mrs. McKinney here to night as usual.

8th. Lovely evening. Mr. C. went down town early this morning & staid until 2, o'clock. I was uneasy for fear he was sick; but it seemed to do him good Oh! if it would be permanent how grateful I *should* & *would* be. Matt at Mrs. Mc helping her with some cake for Will Austin & bride, who are to live with Mrs. Mc. I hope they will have as happy time as the year we had in that little room. I had a general cleaning up it is not often I get my room to do that. Mrs. Harrison & Jamerson here a little while in the evening.

9th. Soon after breakfast an awful looking cloud arose. Matt could not go to Sunday school or church it was raining very soon &

she has a sore throat. I went to church, but had a dreadful time so muddy, few out, no sermon, but prayer meeting, it seemed there was but little spirit in the prayer oh for an awakening among the members. Mr. C. poorly all day.

March 10th. (62) Lovely morning, went directly after breakfast to Dr. Brewers had my tooth filled with rubber until I got well of this bad cold I have; came back & found Mr. C. had gone to the store, he staid until 2 o'clock & seemed quite well. No chill to-day. Mr. Marchmore up here soon this morning came to explain the curious caper he cut here last night, which was—about 9 o'clock some one rang the bell, (Mrs. Mc was undressed, Matt also with dressing gown on, no fire in the parlor). Mr. Marchmore was announced. Matt hurried on her *bib & tucker* Mrs. Mc came in to sleep in my bed, (for we always make preparation for him to be here until near the small hours of the night). Matt walked to the parlor to ask him in when behold—he was not there. He said he created such a stir, he thought he would just slip off. Marchmore like Miss Tish Henderson here in the evening, Matt went down town & got Patty Curd six beautiful dresses. I am going to work to make short dresses for her, wont she be sweet? Mrs. Abbott & Nancy here at night. Mr. Marchmore came home with Matt came in our room & had prayers. What time of night he left it would be hard to say; & was all the time *dead* with the head ache. We slept well to-night, Mr. C. coughed about 5 o'clock & we got up & I wrote up my journal before day.

11th. Beautiful morning. Sent for aunt Ann to spend the day also aunt Martha; cousin Mary came late in the day, Mrs. Junius Robertson here in the morning. Matt took Patty Hart to see Mrs. Nolly & Overton, she almost worships the child, we must try & not think too much of her. I felt so depressed all day it was impossible for me to entertain, & know they must have had a dull time. Oh! me!—it is impossible for me to shake off these feelings. I am so anxious about Mr. Curd; & besides feel so interested in the interest of the South, she dear as the apple of my eyes. [2 lines erased]. Not a word from home; how comforting it would be to be able to pour out my mind into their ears. About 5. o'clock the hack came up for Matt to go to Will Austin's wedding. Mr. Marchmore, Dedmon, Ed Curd & Rickenbaugh went in with her; they got lost & went far out of the way & did not get to Mr. Hook's until 8, o'clock, soon after the ceremony came off, it was a big country wedding.

Mr. C was very much frightened Matt came home that night, she has quite a bad sore throat. Betty Nicholson came in the evening & spent the night; cousin Martha & aunt Martha here until bed time. Mr. C. went down town to-day & staid until 2 o'clock but he still has chills, it is amazing to see his patience. Mrs. Barbour made a long visit this evening made herself very agreeable.

12th. Another lovely day. Mr. C went out again to-day. Mrs. Wells sent him a snack just in time. She & Mr. W have been exceedingly kind to Mr. C. The bridal party came in before Mrs. Mc. expected them. She had fashionable dinner hour, a young lady came in with her. Heard from brother John, dont tell when he can come down; says the Feds are taking up people by lots, & making them stay in, or pay large securities. His feelings are decidedly Southern, wish I could talk with him hope he will be here soon.

13th. Mr. Curd quite feeble, in the house all day, it was a disagreeable day, Matt went to Mrs. McKinney's late in the evening to call on the bride & go from there to prayer meeting. Mrs. Mc was too unwell has a pain in her hip. Mr. Bouland came this morning to spend some time; he is truly one of the salt of the earth, I feel continually reproached for my inconsistency when I am with him, how much more so when I compare my life with my great Pattern; These are days when I need the Grace of God in great power oh! I feel as if my heart would burst; there is nothing but a gloomy future to me oh! God the idea of my dear husband being taken and I left almost crushes me; I cant be blind to his condition & he so patient truly the grace of God is rich unto him. "Oh! that mine eyes were a fountain of tears" I am led to exclaim, & when I look at my dear little baby I think how unconscious she is of what may be her condition before long; & think of my responsibility in raising her alone. Oh! God I am overcome. Give me grace or I die.

14th. Dark gloomy day, not darker out than in to our poor bleeding heart. Mr. C very feeble all day not able to see Mr. Bouland, I sit & watch & wish I could relief but in vain; & poor Matt is a sore trial to him; her brothers have been all in all to her. I wish she would feel to me as a sister. She is as kind as one could be to me, & I miss her so much if away I dont know what I would do without her, I feel so sad [erasure] brother Ed has gone to Jefferson, we have so few in family.

Saturday 15th. Dark & gloomy rather sleety, no body at breakfast table but Matt & I, I feel drawn to her. We were very much alarmed soon this morning. Mr. C awoke & in trying to move his foot it gave him violent pain, made him scream, & he so patient it dont take a slight pain to do that. I sent off for Dr. Abbott directly, he said it must be pneuralgy, sent up some liniment to rub him and gave him some cough medicine, which has good deal morphine he soon became relieved went to sleep took a long nap and awoke much refreshed. After dinner Mr. Bouland came in to see him he had a most satisfactory talk with Mr. C. & advised him to join the church. Oh! shall I ever cease praising my God for this—that He should answer my prayers, & let me see him converted. Glory to God in the highest. I think it will be good for him Mr. B staying here. He slept better than usual to night.

16th.   Beautiful day, was in hopes Mr. C could go to church; but he has been very unwell all day, scarcely able to sit up, it seems so often the case on Sunday he can never go to church; but there is consolation of an ever Present God not confined to places. I trust his grace may be sufficient to his need. Matt went to church in the morning & staid with Mr. C. at night (she is *so kind*) but after going I felt so badly I was pained all the time there, Mr. C used always to be with me & now—I have to be alone, what a trial none can tell but those who have it to endure. I feel like being in sack cloth & ashes. Mr. Robert Dyer here to dinner, Mr. Wilson, Mr. Junius Robinson & lady in the evening. Mr. W sung with us & had prayers, he made a most feeling prayer. Patty Hart has a mighty bad cold, I was so scared last night I gave her some Squills & it must have been too strong she began to vomit & I was afraid I couldn't stop her, she was so sick for some time; but I think will help her. her pa is so anxious for her & looks at her with such tenderness, often says he wishes he was well enough to play with her, he is the best of husbands & fathers. Mr. Dyer told us, they had taken Walker up for what he did not know it will most break Mrs. Dyer's heart. Trouble is abroad in the land truly, at this time, each heart knoweth its own bitterness.

Monday 17th.   Most beautiful morning, Mr. C seems quite well, went down town & staid until 2 o'clock. I dread the morrow after such days with him as this. I had a general fixing of beds, oiled them with coal oil & I tell you they smelt loud, am afraid it will make Mr. C sick. As I had never been to Mrs. Pattons, I thought I would go & see Mrs. James Patton also; so for a great rarity I sent for Mrs. Mc. to stay with Mr. C & I dressed up & started off with

Matt. I felt so out of place fixed up. We went there & then to see Mrs. Finly & Allen the former I think must die with consumption, it pained me to see her. & then came by Mr. Lawther, they expect to go to St. Louis to have something done for Mr. L's leg. Got home before dark, Mr. C went to bed soon after I got back; he slept well until 2 o'clock, I rubbed his feet & he got up & dressed & we sat up over 2 hours. I enjoyed it very much he didnt seem to suffer. I thought I would fix my hoops, but it made me sick to sew them. We got to talking on religion to my great delight said he would join the church very soon. I believe him a genuine Christian. We went to bed after 4 o'clock & slept until six.

18th. Went to Dr. Brewers soon this morning, didnt finish my teeth, began to rain & I was impatient to get home; found Mr. C stupified & I think he is more languid then I ever saw him. Oh Lord my heart aches to look at, or think of him, he has slept all day cant be aroused. Cousin Sue here this evening. So strange that Matt & myself had the same dream about Bro Ed, that he was in very bad health hope it may not come to pass. Matt, Mr. B & bro Ed. went to prayer meeting to-night. I never leave Mr. C alone. Felt so dreadfully oppressed to-night. But I can feel that if Mr. C should be taken, my loss would be his gain; blessed hope.

19th. Mr. C a little better, we are having dreadful weather it makes well people feel badly. Mr. C has missed his chills several day. Mr. Bouland went to see Mr. Fisher; but was back to dinner.

20th. Everything about as usual; my chief happiness is trying to do something for Mr. Curd. Read to him to-day, partly in the Confession of Faith; he seems anxious to hear & have things explained. Miss Matt Patton here this morning.

March 21st. Gloomy, windy day, no body came I dont think. Mr. C still very feeble, did not rest well last night.

22nd. A day ever to be remembered to men & us, Mr. Curd was received into the church. Oh! blessed thought that we are married in the Lord, my prayers have been answered though too faithless I have been. The session met this afternoon & it was very affecting. May we follow after Christ & make him all in all. Mr. Marchmore here this morning, Matt has heard; he had said unkind things & she was very cold in her manners to him. I am sorry she was quite so much so, but think he did wrong; & ought to be made to feel it. I know he will make a grievous complaint about Matt's manner to him; but it will rub off when it gets dry. Cousin Va here

& says Joe has gotten a pass to go out this district & will go to California as soon as possible. Good thing for him to do.

23rd A beautiful morning; Mr. C first thought he might go to church but he grew weaker & was as drowsy as possible all day. Oh! it is so sad to see disease making its inroads day by day & feel there is no help for it; but we have so much to comfort us in his having a hope for the future, we should never cease praising God for this blessed change. For a wonder no one here to-day. Mr. Bouland still with us. I did not go out during the day.

24th Lovely morning Mr. C went down town & staid until dinner we could have gone to cousin Va's, but Ann put Patty's clean dress in wash & she has no other long one that was clean, I was mighty disappointed. Mr. J. Patton & Miss Matt called this morning, am pleased with the former. Like Spring weather to-day so anxious to get the yard & garden fixed.

25th Another pretty day, but Mr. C did not sleep last night & is very feeble to-day didn't get up until 10 o'clock. Cousin Va came over & sat sometime; she said Matt & Henry & Joe Watkins started to St. Louis this morning. Mr. Thompson, Henry's beau went with them as far as St. Aubert. I reckon they will marry. Matt went down yesterday & asked Mary Scott & Miss Lou Baker to come up this evening & meet Will Austin & Lady. We didnt feel like having company; but thought we ought to ask Will Austin up they came early in the evening also Mary Abbott & Matt Hockaday & went away to prayer meeting; so there was not much entertaining to do. Aunt Martha staid here until bed time. I feel so sad it is the greatest trial to try to entertain nowadays, & after all trying dont succeed. Oh! to think of the dear home ones, never hearing from them it is such a severe trial. God help me for this & other trials.

March 26th Mr. Curd Patty & myself went to cousin Va's soon this morning. Mr. Lawther had come from the store scared most to death because his leg had bled. All said he would have been terribly blue if no one had gone in; when he finds himself worse he cries all night; poor man I wish he would come out decidedly on the Lords side; but he will not give up the world as he ought to do. Mr. C seems very comfortable, went home after three o'clock found cousin Mary Abbott & Mrs. Wells there when we got there, & in a little while Mr. Diggs & Thorny came on horse back, the roads are so bad Jinny couldnt come. A Soldier came here Monday for Mr. Bouland to sentence him to appear at the Provost Marshall's office; he had gone to the Country he came home Tuesday, but went away again, I reckon will stay as he is conscientious about taking the oath.[35] I am afraid they will imprison him, these are the times to try men's souls; & how sad to think how many fall away.

27th Mr. Curd walked down with me to the store seemed quite well, I went up to Dr. Brewer's office to have a tooth fixed. He stopped first, in at Aunt Martha's & made her a visit. It is a great comfort to see him better; but I know there is nothing to build upon for to-morrow he may be too feeble to be up. Cousin Va & Mr. L. started to St. Louis this morning I am glad he is gone, kept him & every body in such suspense. He has a lovely day to go.

28th I went directly after breakfast to Brewer's, he finished my tooth at last, but I am afraid it wont look, nor wear well. a most singular morning bright as possible early, but very soon the whole heavens were clouded, it thundered & hailed & rained & was so dark couldnt see to sew for a while. Mr. C got home just before it rained I was so relieved. I found Mrs. Van Doren here, when I got home, she seems to try to talk; but it is evidently an effort, & she has enough to sadden her heart Mr. Van Doren started yesterday to California & left them penniless, a woman with 5 children has no little charge left to herself. Deliver me for being separated from my husband in this way. Jinny Nicholson came in to try & get the horse Joe Watkins rode when he was taken. Snidegor would not give it up, but said she could bid for it at the Auction to-morrow; she & cousin Martha Watkins here this evening. Lightening struck a tree, in Mr. L's yard, to-day.

March 29th Quite a pretty day Mr. C only tolerable did not go out all day. I dont think any one came in or went out. Mr. Diggs here all day. Patty is as sweet as possible & pats the cakes sweet enough to eat her up.

30th A lovely morning cool enough to be pleasant and healthy. I am glad to say Mr. C is well enough to go to church the first time since he has been staying in the house. A day long to be remembered by us all. Mr. Curd made a public profession of religion, there was a large congregation & many with whom he joined in sin, saw him make it God grant it may be blessed. Oh! it did delight my heart, to see him in his weakness give himself up to God. His whole character is change he is as patient & gentle as it is possible to be, even in his extreme weakness. Cousin Sarah & Mr. Robert Dyer came here from church to dinner. No preaching at the Methodist church. Mr. Bouland not returned. Mr. Marchmore excelled himself in preaching to-day his subject was Heaven one of a series of three am sorry I couldnt hear them all. Matt said he acquitted himself finely at night. He was here Sunday night until nearly 11, o'clock has never had a private chat with Matt yet; but I think is quite anxious. He eyes her closely to see how she takes things.

31st Mr. C seemed so well early, was calling me up & walked to the stable before breakfast; we thought of going to Judge Hockaday's, but it clouded up & looked as if it would rain directly. Mr. Diggs started home. Matt went to Brewers & staid until after 12 o'clock & came back with whom—but Mr. Marchmore; a very poor prospect for dinner one of scraps—but we had some oysters & Matt made some oyster soup which with some eggs & what we had made the table look quite full of dishes. Mr. M played with Patty, & very dryly remarked she couldnt be well as her tongue was very much furred—it was with milk he looked as if he didnt mean any thing; but there is no telling. While at dinner Mr. & Mrs. Kerr came, of course there was much great talking with Mr. K & M. They staid until late & went down town in the rain. Mr. M is so imprudent his throat bled a good deal last night, & to-day he is out in the rain. It is so sad to see so young a minister thus afflicted. Oh! the sorrow that is in the land; surely all must feel the nothingness & vanity of earthly things. Teach me to let go this world, & look only to the future. Oh! my heart aches.

April 1st Raining early this morning & continued during the day. Mr. C very feeble sleeping all day; he seems gradually to be wasting away overwhelming thought; but I cant be blind to it. My only comfort is the hope he has of the future, he is truly consecrated I believe, & our loss will be his gain, but my God! how can I bear the thought of seeing him taken oh! I have not grace to say as I should Thy will be done. What would I not give to have my dear father with me, & my other friends; he has always been with me in trouble; but not even a line of comfort from him can I have, God grant that these bitter hours may work out for me a far more exceeding & Eternal weight of glory. My own family, I mean Matt & brother Ed, are & do all that kindness can suggest; but it is natural for us to feel a yearning for those who have been with us from infancy. I dont know what I would do without Matt she is all a sister could be.

2nd Clear & then cloudy all day with much wind. Matt & Mrs.

Kerr went to Mr. Hendersons' early this morning to spend the day. I am selfish about Matt leaving at all. I feel so lonely not lonely either; but that I want some one in sympathy with me. Mr. C has been drowsy and feeble all day. Patty some what fretful for her to be. Dr. Abbott here in the morning. After dinner Mr. Wells and Grant came but Mr. C was so feeble they left very soon. Cousin Mary, Dr. Abbott, Mrs. McKinney & Mr. Austin came during the evening. Mr. A. went away soon, the others staid. Mr. & Mrs. Kerr supped with Major Nolly did not get back until 9, o'clock. Mr. Marchmore came up right early thinking he would have a good talk with Matt, but he was *"set aback"* by seeing Dr. & Mrs. Abbott here, his lower lip hung still lower when he came in & saw matters as they were. He staid until 11, o'clock. Mr. Kerr saw him also did Matt.

3rd   Beautiful morning Mr. & Mrs. Kerr left this morning I am sorry they couldn't stay longer. Mr. C rode down town but it did not help him he went to try the effect he is still drowsy. Tina Watkins & Matt Lawther here. Mr. L. had to have another operation on his leg he has had a serious time with his leg. I hope it may be sanctified to him. May he be as godly as he has been worldly. Cousin Sue & Mr. Tuttle here to night; it so hard to talk to any body, for entertainment. I have neither subject nor heart.

April 4th   This has been a long day not 8 o'clock yet. Mr. C has been unusually feeble all day; it seems to me he has declined very much in the last week; but is as patient & composed as possible truly grace has done wonders for him. Mrs. Vaughters here this evening she has a cancer & is just getting better from having it burnt. Mrs. Snell & Mrs. Abbott came presently. Came in the room but I think it was not comfortable to Mr. C—he took his supper soon, & went to bed & is now sleeping pleasantly hope he will have a good night. I feel unusually depressed to night; Mr. C seems to be extremely weak, Oh! how (gloomy) to look at him, it makes me feel; he only weighs 121 lbs.

From April 4th to   [May 20th scratched through, 1862 added later.] Mr. C grew worse very rapidly, I had not the heart, nor the time to write, we went to St. Louis the first of April; he stood the trip better than we had feared, Matt went as far as the river, Mr. Hook went to St. Louis with us. We staid at Mr. Moore's a night & part of a day, the wind was high in the morning, there was no boat to be had, at last the wind lulled, we put mattress & comforts in the boat, Mr. Hook sat at his head & thus we crossed the river, he said he had not been so comfortable for a long time, it began to rain soon after we got across; but he did not get wet, every body tried to do something for his comfort, the cars came, we got on, & off to St. Louis—the rode is miserably rough, I feared he would be shaken to death, got to St. Louis at half past 7 o'clock; went to the Wood's House, because the Keeper used to live in Fulton, & knew Mr. C; he slept well that night—went to breakfast next morning but soon after it, was taken with dysentery, which confined him to his bed—this was Saturday. [ink changes] 1862.

June 15th 1863 I have thought an innumberable number of times I would write in my journal but when I made the attempt, each time my heart was too full to write, & now I feel as if it were *brim* full of sorrow oh! God thou only canst tell my sorrow. Help me to keep from murmuring. Since I last wrote, time to *me* has not been measured by the brief span of days & weeks; but it has draged its *"weary length along"* with such heaviness, that I can scarcely be convinced that only 13 months have passed away since the death of my dear husband. Oh! God what hours of gloom & thick darkness, of loneliness bordering at times on despair, of weariness, feeling at night as if my days, had been of toil, & awakening with the same crushing consciousness, that I was widowed, a feeling which if language were exhausted no idea could be given of its full import. God & myself only know what I have felt to be—a *widow*. On which side I turn I find reminders of him. My heart continually feels burdened, & I long for him in whose ears, I poured out my soul, & who was ever ready to rejoice with me in my rejoicings and mourn with me in my sorrows. Truly in the brief span of life spent with him, my joys were doubled, my sorrows divided. God saw that my affection was too set on that earthly temple, that I was loving the world too well & He came & by a slow, lingering disease, He made my dear husband, prostrate, thus in his mercy designing to prepare me & him, for the final stroke. Yes I know that he was prepared, that my loss was his gain; but I cannot say I was, though I knew he could not last long, yet his death came unexpectedly to me; and I could but feel how alleviating, and comforting it would have been had he been conscious of being at home, and could have spoken to us, giving that heart-rending, yet from the dieing, to the living most touching word—good-bye. Although 13 months have passed away, yet I feel my loneliness, my inestimable loss, my need

of him, my indescribable bereavement, not to have abated, but
increased, I feel that each day brings with it greater need of him. It
is true his family have done & been all that friends & kindness
could suggest; but there is a void made by his death, which the
dearest friend of earth could not fill. I feel I need more grace to
sustain me & I too often murmur at this Providence, would I could
see it, & improve it as God intended it should be, for I know He will
accomplish his design, & if this affliction be not improved he will
come with some other.

June 15th   Monday morning, awoke depressed & that feeling
has deepened, feel a want of interest in every thing as if there was
nothing for me to live for, and but for the great interest in my
darling little Patty, I should be undone. She is the source of greatest comfort to me, talking now, and as bright and winning in her
ways as she can be. God has been merciful to spare her, may her
life be precious in his sight. Mr. Marchmore has been staying with
us. He spoke of going to Columbia to-day; but did not get off. Mr.
Curtis is afraid of losing his horses. I feel so sorry for him; he is
sorely tried. I feel so disturbed at the thought of his going away, &
hope that he may still live amongst us. He has been such a comfort
to us in our affliction, & shall miss him so much. I wish I could have
some fixed purpose; but I feel there is nothing to be done, & can
loiter & idle away the day without any thing being accomplished. I
am condemned for my waste of time; but the more I try to guard
my feelings, the stronger they seem to become. Another source of
trouble I never receive a letter from home not one since November. How many changes, since then to families whose sons
have been given to their country. I have ceased to look for letters
from home. I will write no more, for were I to fill this book, it
would be but a repetition of sorrow's tale.

[At this point the daily entries end. There are nineteen blank
pages. On the last six pages Sam hand copied a series of poems, as
follows.]

Both Sides Of The Shield

1 - Shade in Light;

Light! emblem of all good & joy!
Shade! emblem of all ill!
And yet in this strange mingled life
    We need the shadow still.
A lamp with softly shaded light,
To soothe and spare the tender sight,
        Will only throw
        A brighter glow
Upon our looks and works below.

We could not bear unchanging day,
    However fair its light.
Ere long the wearied eye would hail
As boon untold, the evening pale
    The solace of the night.
And who would prize our Summer glow,
If Winter gloom, they did not know?
        Or rightly praise
        The glad Spring rays,
Who never saw our rainy days?

How gratified in Arabian plain
    Of white and sparkling sand,
The shadow of a mighty rock
    Across the weary land.
And where the tropic glories rise,
Responsive to the fiery skies,
        We could not dare
        To meet the glare.
Or blindness were our bitter share.

Where is the soul so meek and pure
    Who through his earthly days
Life's fullest sun shine could endure
    In clear and cloudless blaze
The sympathetic eye would dim,

And others pine unmarked by him,
  Were no chill shade
  Around him laid
And light of joy could never fade.

He who the light-commanding word
  First spake and formed the eye,
Knows what that wondrous eye can bear,
And tempers with providing care,
By cloud and night all hurtful glare,
  By shadows ever nigh
Lo in all wise and loving ways,
He blends the darkening of our days,
    To win our sight
    From scenes of night
To seek the True and only light.

We need some shadow o'er our bliss,
  Lest we forget the Giver:
So often in our deepest joy,
There comes a solemn shiver;
We could not tell from whence it came,
The subtle cause we cannot name:
    Its twilight fall,
    May well recall
Calm thought of him Who gave us all.

There are who all undazzled tread
  Awhile the sunniest plain;
But they have sought the blessed shade
By one great Rock of Ages made
  A sure safe rest to gain.
Unshaded light of earth soon blinds,
To light of heaven sincerest minds;
    Oh, envy not
    A cloudless lot!
We ask indeed we know not what.

So is it here, so is it now?
Not always will it be!
There is a land that needs no shade,

A morn will rise which cannot fade.
And we like flamed-robe angels made
    That Glory soon may see.
No cloud upon its radiant joy,
No shadow o'er its bright employ
        No sleep no night
        But perfect sight
The Lord our Everlasting Light.

                2- Light in Shade!

There is no rose without a thorn
Who has not found it true
And known that griefs of gladness borne
Our footsteps still persue.

That in the grandest harmony
The strongest discords rise
The brightest bow we only see
Upon the darkest skies?

No Thornless rose, so more & more
Our pleasant hopes are laid,
Where waves this sable legend o'er
A still sepulchral shade.

But Faith and Love with Angel might
Break up Lifes dismal tomb
Transmiting into golden light
The words of leaden gloom.

Reversing all this funeral pace
White garments they disclose,
Their happy song floats full & long
No Thorn without a rose!

No shadow, but its sister light
Not far away must burn:
No weary night, but morning bright
Shall follow in its turn.

No chilly snow, but safe below
A million buds are sleeping;
No wintry days, but fair spring rays
Are swiftly onward sweeping.

No burning glare of Summer air
But fullest is the shade;
And shady fruit bends every shoot
Because the blossoms fade.

No note of sorrow, but shall melt
In sweetest chord impressed;
No labor, all too pressing felt
But ends in quiet rest.

No sigh but from the harp above
Soft echoing tones shall win;
No heart wound, but the Lord of love
Shall pour his comfort in.

No withering hopes, while loving best
Thy father's chosen way;
No anxious care, for He will bear
Thy burdens every day.

Thy claim to rest on Jesu's breast
All weariness shall win;
No heart wound, but the Lord of love
Shall pour his comfort in.

No withering hopes, while loving best
Thy father's chosen way;
No anxious care, for He will bear
Thy burdens every day.

Thy claim to rest on Jesu's breast
All weariness shall be;
And pain thy portal to this heart
Of wondrous sympathy.

No conflict but the King's own hand

Shall end the glorious strife.
No death, but leads thee to the land
Of everlasting life.

Sweet seraph voices Faith & love:
Sing on within our hearts
This strain of music from above
Till we have learnt our parts.

Until we see your alchemy
On all that years disclose
And taught by you still find it true
No Thorn without a Rose.

To the Loved & lost

My heart in the grave my love,
Oh! let it there remain;
In life I gave it, & in death
Thou shalt the gift retain.

And faithful to thy memory
I'll ceasless homage pay;
For blissful moments of wedded love
Too swiftly passed away.

Thou saidst that we had got to part
That death was drawing nigh;
Oh! who can tell the *hopeless* grief
With which I saw thee die?

Behold thine eyes of love & light
Dimmed with the mist of death;
Received upon my quivering lips
Thy last expiring breath.

Oh! what a fine & generous soul
Did death in thine set free;
Oh! what a *wealth* of *priceless love*
I've *lost* in *losing thee.*

Truth, genius, virtue, beauty, all
That lent a charm to life,
Lie buried in thy timeless grave,
My lost, my cherished wife.

And I will plant thy grave with flowers,
And watch this growth with care—
The same as used to win thy love
The fragrant, bright, and fair.

The earliest violet of the spring,
With lovelier hue shall bloom,
When watered by affections tear,
That falls on beauty's tomb.

Look down, then from the realms of light
If such be heavens decree
Watch all our ways when perils press
Our guardian angel be.

Yes whisper with thy seraph voice,
Thy loved ones will obey;
Fence guide us through earth's clouded path,
To heavens effulgent day.

These severed souls whose early faith,
Was pledged in changeless love
Shall reunite—no more to part—
In God's bright home above.

Mozart's Last Piece of Composition

Spirit thy labor is o'er
Thy term of Probation is run,
Thy steps are now bound for the untrodden shore,
And the race of immortals begun.

Spirit! Look not on the strife
Or the pleasures of earth with regret—

Pause not on the threshold of limitless life,
To mourn for the day that is set.

Spirit! no fetters can bind,
No wicked have power to molest;
There the weary, like thee—the wretched shall find,
A heaven—a mansion of rest.

Spirit! how bright is the road,
For which thou art now on the wing!
Thy home, it will be with thy Saviour & God,
Their loud hallelujahs to sing.

The False Spirit

O, why must the strains of my heart be so sad
When its golden strings tremulously heave,
And like the wild notes from the death-stricken bird,
But sorrow and agony breathe.

In vain do I now touch the soul-breathing strings,
And awaken a livelier air;
The low voice of sorrow its wild wailing brings,
And turn all its notes to despair.

For the spirit that dwelt in its every part,
And breathed in its every strain,
Has vanished! now leaving that trembling harp
To quiver and vibrate with pain.

I took the lone harp and again touched the chords,
And its false spirit strove to forget;
But still every breath, with its music & words,
Awoke fond remembrances yet.

They sang of that form on which angels might gaze
And envy the loveliness there;
Of those bright starry eyes with their silvery rays,
And that brow with its dark midnight hair.

And as they thus sang, & how soft and how clear
The melody floated around;
'Twere sweet as if Annie's low voice mingled there,
And whispered in every sound.

And I sung then of truth, and quickly the strain
Grew harsher each word that I spoke;
And when I had breathed her sworn vows o'er again
The straining chord quivered—and broke!

That harp and my heart are so closely entwined
That they tremble and vibrate as one;
And the same hand that rends its soft strings will find
The chords of my heart are undone.

Fulton December 26th. 1862

The Bereaved One (Copied Dec: 26th. 1862)   Bright and mild as
                                               Spring, but the sun
                                               is but a mockery to
                                               my sad heart.

He knelt beside the grave of her whose life
Had seemed a very portion of his own;
And, as the evening zephyrs kissed his cheek
And fanned his burning brow, he prayed for strength.
And resignation to endure this trial
Of faith that he was called to undergo.

Oh! if there is one spot on earth that seems
As though 'twere nearer heaven than all the rest
One sacred spot, where the hearts offering
Goes up more swiftly to the thrones of Him
Who hears & answers prayer, it is beside
The grave of one we dearly loved in life.

The sun had set behind a silver cloud—
The birds had sung their evening hymns of praise,
And now with folded wing slept quietly,

While the bright moon beams softly stole to earth
Casting a mellow light on all around,
And the stars waking from their noonday sleep
Came out to deck the canopy of heaven.

But none of these the stricken mourner saw;
His thoughts were with the spirit of the dead.
For twelve short months the dear one had been lent
To cheer him with her looks & words of love;
And then a bright winged seraph, who was sent
To take her guardian angels's place, while He
Went up to worship, fell in love with her
Who seemed too pure and good to linger here
And carried her above.
                            'Tis ever thus—
The lovely flowers that most we cherish here
Round which our fond affections closely twine,
Are snatched away by unseen angel's hands
To be transplanted to the world above.

Fulton December 26th. 1862

[On the last lined page, the following is written:]

Mr. C died April 28th. 1862 buried 30th. Funeral text Job 23rd 21st
        Preached by Mr. S. A. Marchmore[36]

Patti Curd died September 5th. 1863 Funeral text 2nd Kings 4th.
    26th. Preached by Mr. S. A. Marchmore[37]

                    In Memoriam

            Another little form asleep
                And a little spirit gone,
            Another little voice is hushed
                And a little angel born.
            Two little feet are on the way
                To the home beyond the skies

And our hearts are like the voice that comes
　　When a strain of music dies.

A pair of little baby shoes
　　And a lock of golden hair,
The toy our little darling loved
　　And the dress she used to wear,
The little grave in the sunny nook
　　Where the flowers love to grow
And these are all of the little hopes
　　That came three years ago.

The birds will sit in the branch above
　　And sing a requiem
To the beautiful little sleeping form
　　That used to sing to them,
But never again will the little lips
　　To their song of love reply;
For that silvery voice is blending with
　　The minstrelsy on high.

[Finally on the last unlined page of the journal, Sam wrote the following:]

Died in Fulton 1864
Mrs. Wilson died July 18th. 7.O'clock A M
Willie Tuttle died July 19th. 2.35 A M
Archie Ryley died July 25th. 4.50 A M
Mrs. Mills died July 26th. 12.20 A M
John Nesbit died July 26th. 9 P M
Minnie Henderson died July 29th. 1.35 A M
Emily Patton died July 30th. 3.30 A M
Miss Lizzie Scott died August 6th. 3 P M
Mr. Robert Grant died August 13th. 5.15 A M
Mrs. McClanahan died August 14th. 2.10 PM
Mr. Dedmons child died August 27th. A M
Mrs. Alice McClellan died August 30th. 5.30 A M
Mr. Meals child died August 31st. 4.30 A M

Miss Lizzie Smith died September 6th
Mr. Wilson's child died October 5th.

Callaway
Miss Herring Aug [unreadable]
Jimmie Nicholson Sept. 3rd

Booneville
Mrs. Lavinia Bell Aug.

Notes
To
The Diary

1. The Fulton Presbyterian church was an Old School Presbyterian Church. Its theology was purely Calvinistic and up until the end of the century Session minutes regularly recorded vigorous opposition to profanity, drinking, and all forms of dancing and theatre. The church history lists the membership in 1860 at 315, and although revivals were very successful in promoting conversions, no new members were taken in during the next two years.

The "Fulton trouble" evidently was rooted in a disagreement between the church's minister, the Rev. Dr. William W. Robertson, and the president of Westminster College, the Rev. Dr. S. S. Laws. The outcome was that Dr. Robertson ceased his church ministry in April 1860, but rancor and division in the congregation lingered on through the war period. The Rev. Dr. S. A. Mutchmore (note spelling) served the church as a supply minister until 1863, when he gave up the work because of ill health. At this time a letter from the Session noted, "Your stay among us has been in troublous times and surrounded by untoward circumstances." Ovid Bell, *The First Presbyterian Church, Fulton, Missouri* (Privately published, 1948).

2. Tom Curd's "ungodliness" is problematic. The Curd family in Virginia had a long history of staunch Presbyterianism. Edwin Curd, Tom's brother, was a long-time deacon in the Fulton church. Although Sam indicates that Tom does not "convert" and unite with the church until March, 1862, Tom's newspaper obituary will record that he "has been a member of the Presbyterian church for some length of time; in which relations he lived an honored and exemplary member until his death." This evidence strongly suggests that Sam may have been using her supposed

more religious nature as a female to assert power within her marriage.

3. Tom and Sam Curd are building a house in Fulton; in the meantime they are boarding with Mrs. McKinney. It is interesting that this is the first mention in the diary of the new house since a woman's sphere was the domestic scene.

4. Sam's view of Bled Karns' use of chloroform seems less than sympathetic. There was a long tradition within Christian churches that saw women's suffering in childbirth as part of God's intention for humankind. When James Y. Simpson, a professor of obstetrics at the University of Glasgow, proposed in the 1840s to use chloroform to relieve the pain of childbirth, a clergyman called the anesthetic "a decay of Satan" and recited God's injunction against women: "I will greatly multiply your pain in childbearing; in pain you shall being forth children." Although Queen Victoria's use of chloroform in childbirth in the 1850s helped to make the drug more acceptable, opposition on religious and other grounds remained. Roy P. Finney, *The Story of Motherhood* (New York: Leveright Publishing Corp., 1937), p. 179.

5. The Mite party and, later, the Mite Society that Sam refers to is probably the women's missionary society. A mite is a small sum of money, referring to the biblical story of the widow's mite (Mark 12:41-44), in which a poor widow gave everything she had—two mites—to Jesus.

Beginning in 1860 women's foreign missionary societies were formed in many American churches. They collected money for foreign missions in "mite boxes." These mission societies collected thousands of dollars as well as building regional and national grass-roots organizations of church women.

6. "The children" referred to here are probably Mrs. McKinney's three sons, Lewis W. (age 18), Charles R. (age 14), and Geo. C. (age 9). All three boys are listed in the 1860 census as living in the household headed by Mary A. McKinney. In fact, the census lists ten people as living in the house in the spring or summer of 1860. In addition to the three boys there were: Mrs. McKinney (age 49), with a personal estate valued at $300; Thomas Curd (age 37), a merchant who owned $30,000 worth of real estate and had a personal estate worth $15,000; Samuella Curd (age 26); Mattie Curd (age 24); Samuel Watson (age 21), a dry goods clerk; Edwin Curd (age 29), merchant; and William Austin (age 22), a dry goods

clerk. From the diary, one would have little knowledge that the house in which Sam, Tom, Matt, and Mrs. Mc lived was so crowded. This is one example of Sam's diary revealing the way in which she ordered her world. One suspects that, for Sam, these other people did not exist as an important part of her world.

7. The "College" was Westminster College. Founded in 1851 as Fulton College, it was chartered as Westminster College in 1853. This "disturbance" that Sam mentions would lead to the resignation of the College President, Rev. S. S. Laws and other faculty. Although the College continued to operate throughout the war, this incident and the uncertainties of wartime made operation difficult. In 1861-62 the college enrolled forty-three students; by 1863-64, enrollment had increased to more than a hundred. See William W. Parrish, *A History of Missouri, 1860-1875*, Vol. III (Columbia: University of Missouri Press, 1973), p. 83.

8. Mishap probably means miscarriage. In August of the previous year, "Cousin Sue's baby" had died. When the *Callaway County History* was written in 1884, Susan Dyer had six living children. The high birthrate in the nineteenth century was due to several factors, including insufficient knowledge of birth control methods and an emphasis on the role of women as mothers.

9. She probably means a "menagerie," a collection of wild or strange animals kept in cages for exhibition. It is unclear whether Sam thinks the crowd is similar to the animals or to the observers, but it is evident that Sam does not enjoy being in public in mixed crowds.

10. Religious publications in the nineteenth century were numerous, aimed particularly at people like Sam, who felt the necessity to "improve the day" by reading religious materials. The particular book Sam mentions is not certain. The most likely candidates are books by Archibald Alexander (1772-1815), either *Thoughts on Religious Experience*, published and reprinted numerous times in Philadelphia by the Presbyterian board of publications, or *A Brief Outline of the Evidences of the Christian Religion*, published and reprinted numerous times between 1825 and 1851 by the American Sunday School Union.

11. The Crittenden Compromise was proposed by Kentucky Whig Senator John J. Crittenden to the Senate on Dec. 18, 1860. It was an attempt to prevent secession and civil war by compromis-

ing the slavery issue. On Dec. 22 a special Senate committee of thirteen members voted against the most important provisions, 7 to 6. In Jan., 1861 Stephen A. Douglas proposed that the Compromise be submitted to a popular referendum. This was not done, nor was the Compromise brought before the Senate for a vote. It is unclear what Sam's news about the Compromise was.

12. Sam is referring to railroad cars when she says "cars."

13. Of all the women mentioned in Sam's diary, Aunt Mary seems to be the one to whom Sam feels closest. Sam talks about being impatient to see her older sister, Jane, but there is little evidence in the diary of warmth at the meetings. Aunt Mary, on the other hand, creates an ambience of ease, quiet, and happiness, despite having ten children living in her house and living in "an ugly little place." Sam and Aunt Mary spend the four days "talking busily." We have the feeling that Aunt Mary is a surrogate mother for Sam as well as the model of a good wife and mother.

14. The references to Fanny Gaines and Seaton Linsley are problematic. The couple was married May 2, 1860, the day before Sam's own marriage. Now, eleven months later, the Linsley's have a baby. Several days later, Sam notes carefully that Fanny's baby is two months old.

15. The firing on Ft. Sumpter took place on the previous day, April 12, and "extras" announcing news of the engagement were distributed in Richmond on the twelfth. The popular demonstration that Sam mentions here did not occur until the thirteenth. The *Richmond Daily Dispatch* described the celebration as "one of the wildest, most enthusiastic and irrepressible expressions of heartfelt and exuberant joy on the part of the people generally, that we have ever known to be the case before in Richmond." Quoted by Emory M. Thomas, *The Confederate State of Richmond: A Biography of the Capital* (Austin, Texas: University of Texas Press, 1971), p. 6.

16. Actually, the Convention had voted for succession two days earlier, on April 17th, but the news was kept secret until the 19th.

17. During the early months of preparation for war, Richmond was the scene of confusion, gaiety, and frivolity as well as serious attempts at organization and discipline. In *The Confederate State of Richmond*, Emory M. Thomas, pp. 36-38, presents some vivid eyewitness accounts of the scene:

"The drilling, of which there was literally no end, was simply funny. Maneuvers of the most utterly impossible sort were carefully taught to the men. Every amateur officer had his own pet system of tactics, and the effect of the incongruous teachings, when brought out in battalion drill, closely resembled that of the music at Mr. Bob Sawyer's party, where each guest sang the chorus to the tune he knew best." [George Cary Eggleston, *A Rebel's Recollection* (New York: G. P. Putnam's Sons, 1905), p. 64.] The horseless adjutant of a cavalry regiment summarized a common predicament in the young army in a letter to his mother: "I have no uniform and no sabre yet. I conduct Dress Parade in my grey pants and blue coat and borrow a sabre from some one on the sick list. If we should receive marching orders I can probably obtain a horse and sabre in this way and march with the regiment." ["T" to Mother, May 15, 1861, Kate Mason Rowland Papers, Confederate Museum, Richmond, Va.]

Throughout May and June of 1861 the troops poured into the city. Volunteers came armed with shotguns, bowie knives, muskets, or squirrel guns. As soon as practicable the companies were mustered into the Confederate service. Then the men drilled, loafed, and awaited orders dispatching them to a probable front.

Elite corps such as the Washington Artillery from New Orleans joined the local "Grays" and "Blues" (Richmond Light Infantry Blues). The young Louisianians with Edward, their French chef from Victor's Restaurant, were popular guests at a round of teas and dances in the city. In the many companies composed of the wealthy and prominent, "whenever a detail was made for cleaning the campground, the men detailed regarded themselves as responsible for the proper performance of their task by their servants, and uncomplainingly took upon themselves the duty of sitting on the fence and superintending the work." [Eggleston, *Rebel's Recollections*, p. 73] Women and girls made regular visits to the camps bearing cakes and other delicacies. Reviews and parades in camp, parties and the theater in the city, added to the gaiety of the season. The horseless cavalry officer reassured his mother about the rigors of army life: "We have had two horseraces this week gotten up by way of amusement. The soldiers using their own horses. You know we are quartered at the Ashland Race-Course. On Friday the officers give a military ball to which $500 have already been subscribed by the different companies. You ask how we live. We occupy a very nice house that belongs to the racing club and have a mess of eighteen or twenty and a caterer who was one of the proprietors of a hotel in Richmond before he joined the army, we of course live well." ["T" to Mother, June 18, 1861.] Enlisted men did not fare so well. For the most part, they lived in tents and subsisted on a diet of bacon, bread, and coffee. Nevertheless, uniforms concealed the marks of social class, and "regardless of social distinction, or castes of society, the barriers which hedge familiar intercourse were broken down, and the man was almost forgotten in the soldier." [Sallie Brock Putnam, *Richmond during the War: Four Years of Personal Observation* New York: G. W. Carleton and Co., 1867, p. 32.] These were the gala days when the excitement of war was enjoyable in Richmond. One diarist, Mary Boykin Chesnut, wife of a South Carolina provisional congressman, recorded: "Noise of drums, tramp of marching regiments all day long, rattling artillery wagons, bands of music, friends from every quarter coming in. We ought to be miserable and anxious, and yet these are pleasant days. Perhaps we are unnaturally exhilarated and excited." [Mary Boykin Chestnut, *A Diary from Dixie*. Edited by Ben Ames Williams. Boston: Houghton Mifflin Co., 1961, p. 75.]

Sam Curd's father's house, located on the northeast corner of Grace and Madison Streets, was three city blocks away from the Old Fair Grounds where many of the troops were stationed. She is, literally, at the center of this excitement. The lack of detail in the diary about the dramatic events around her is remarkable.

18. An agreement about Virginia's union with the Confederacy was drawn up on the 24th, but the Convention did not ratify the agreement until the next day, April 25th.

19. Lewis's identity is uncertain, but his "place" at the Spottswood Hotel put him at the center of activity. At this time President Jefferson Davis and his family were residing at the Spottswood Hotel, and until more permanent facilities were made available, the Spottswood was the center of the Confederacy.

20. This is the battle at Big Bethel Church, near Hampton. The *Richmond Dispatch* reported that 4000 Union troops were engaged by 1100 Confederates. The reporter echoed Sam's view of the providential victory: "Does not the hand of God seem manifest in this war?" The commander of the Confederate forces, Col. John

Magruder, reported that the Union force was twice the size of the Confederate force and put the casulties at eight for the Confederates, seventy-six for the Federals.

21. "Dutch Soldiery" refers to the German immigrants who settled largely in the area around St. Louis. These Germans were relatively recent immigrants; they were overwhelmingly pro-Union and anti-slavery. Sam's use of the word "scamps" to describe the Germans indicates the ethnic prejudice felt by Americans, particularly southerners, from the more "civilized" southern states.

22. "Mr. C says he never was so welcomed home." This is a high compliment to Sam's skill as a wife in creating a wide social network for herself and her husband after their marriage. She has done her job of visiting well and he recognizes her success.

23. This is the first direct mention in the diary of Sam's pregnancy, which is called "sickness." Sam is approximately seven and a half months pregnant at this point. Her complaints about not being able to walk to her "own" church in Richmond and her concern about not having clothes become more understandable, as does her comment in the diary on the previous Sunday: ". . . at first thought I would not go to church, but then felt, I was doing wrong probably & ought to make a sacrifice of my feelings & go, so I did, but it was a trial. Mr. C hates for me to feel this way." According to Carl N. Degler, *At Odds*, pp. 59-60, pregnancy was rarely mentioned by nineteenth-century women in their letters or diaries and they were hesitant to be seen in public places when visibly pregnant.

24. Sam's appraisal of political sympathies in Fulton and the surrounding area is incorrect. In the Presidential election of November, 1860, Abraham Lincoln had received 15 out of the 2,632 votes cast in Callaway County, in which Fulton was located. Callaway, the fourth largest slave-holding county in the state, was a notoriously conservative county, popularly referred to at the end of the war as the "Kingdom of Callaway." Callaway County, along with Boone County to the west and Audrain County to the north, were at the heart of an area of Missouri popularly known as "Little Dixie." The Presbyterian churches in Missouri also tended to be pro-South in their sympathies. After the General Assembly resolved to uphold the Federal government in 1861, the Synod of Missouri resolved "that the action of the General Assembly was

unscriptural, unconstitutional, unwise, and unjust. We, therefore solemnly protest against it, and declare it of no binding force upon this Synod or upon members of the Presbyterian Church within our bounds."

On the other hand, election returns indicate that most people were not strongly pro-war, wishing to compromise rather than fight. It may have been this compromising stance that made Sam attribute pro-Union sympathies to the local citizens. See Bell, *The Story of the Kingdom of Callaway*, p. 5; Parrish, *History of Missouri*, III, 117 and 264; and Lewis G. Vander Velde, *The Presbyterian Churches and the Federal Union, 1861-1869* (Cambridge: Harvard University Press, 1932), pp. 99 and 215.

25. State finances in Missouri were in bad condition by this time. In May, 1861, the General Assembly had granted all of the funds reserved for the state's schools and charitable institutions to the state militia. Fulton had two such institutions: the Deaf and Dumb School, called the "Institute", and the Insane Asylum. As a consequence of the state's financial situation, asylums such as the two in Fulton ceased to function. In most cases, the inmates were simply released.

26. General Fremont proclaimed martial law for the entire state on August 30. The proclamation made anyone found with arms liable to court-martial; anyone found guilty would be shot. Anyone who took up arms against the Union would forfeit all property including slaves, who would be freed. Although President Lincoln quickly rescinded both of these measures, Fremont's proclamation served to intensify the bitter factionalism which characterized Missouri during the war and after. Martial law remained in effect in Missouri until 1865.

27. Sam's use of "dependence" seems ironic. She assumes that mobility is independence.

28. Sam's comments here are intriguing. That Mrs. B looks "interesting" probably means that she is visibly pregnant. Sam seems to have divided emotions about Mr. B. She is envious that the Barbours are moving to "Dixie," but at the same time, Sam disapproves of Mr. B's lack of employment which she calls "fickle."

29. From this point in the diary, erasures become more frequent; in all, there are nine passages that are erased or inked out. We can only speculate when the erasures were made and why. What did Sam write that she later expunged? Most of the erasures

are so complete that nothing can be read, but in this one, of the five and a half lines erased a few phrases or words remain that hint at the original message's content: "I admit . . . have . . . not one *friend* . . . with me . . . none . . . but Mr. Curd . . . nobody . . . but it useless to. . . . " Sam's resentment at her confinement to the house with the baby while Matt and Mr. Curd are free to go out into the community becomes amplified into feelings of isolation and friendlessness and, finally, despair at the futility of complaining. The passage denies the picture of domestic felicity that Sam tries so hard to maintain and this may be the reason it was later erased.

30. Brigadier General Chester Harding, Jr., the leader of this force, wrote that he took 650 men to Fulton. His opinion of the sentiments of Fulton and surrounding Callaway County contradicts Sam's: "That whole region is thoroughly disloyal. There is no faith to be placed in anything but the fear of Rebels. On our return a single individual rode up within two hundred yards of our advance guard and fired at it, and this is an indication of the universal feeling there. There are not two hundred Union men in the county of Callaway." Quoted by Bell, *The Story of the Kingdom of Callaway*, p. 21.

31. Robert Dyer's drinking is mentioned several times in the diary; on September 22, it is referred to as "his bad habits." Sam notes the effect on Mrs. Dyer.

32. Dr. Abbott evidently diagnosed Mr. Curd as tubercular; Sam had earlier feared that he was "prey to consumption." His cough and the "cold" that has lingered on for over a year, support this diagnosis. Other symptoms such as the chills, fevers, and sweats, and the use of quinine as medicine, suggest that Mr. Curd was also a victim of "fever and ague," a generic name for a malarial disease frequently found in low-lying newly settled areas before standing water was drained off.

33. Sam's treatment of Henry's childbirth indicates that Henry may be a slave living in Sam's house: (1) the 24-hour labor is treated rather cavalierly; (2) "grunting" is not a word used to describe Sam's or her friends' labors—it is certainly not appropriate to white, middle class, nineteenth-century women; (3) there is no indication that Sam leaves her house to hear the "grunting;" and (4) calling the baby a "man child" indicates his eventual status—at 12 years of age a male slave became a man and was more valu-

able; elsewhere in the diary Sam calls her friends' male children "boys."

34. Sam's reticence to become too attached to her child for fear the child would die was probably common among mothers of small children at this time. In the twenty-two months since Sam began her diary, she has mentioned the deaths of at least eight children of her friends. At least one of Sam's own younger siblings died when Sam was a child.

35. All ministers were required to take an oath of loyalty to the Union.

36. This reference is probably to Job 21.23: "One dieth in his full strength, being wholly at ease and quiet." (King James Version.)

37. II Kings 4.26: "Run now, I pray thee to meet her, and say unto her, Is it well with thee? is it well with thy husband? is it well with the child? And she answered, It is well." (King James Version.)

Epilogue

What happened to Sam? Was the rest of her life "but a repetition of sorrow's tale?" We don't know. A tombstone in the Curd family plot in Hillcrest Cemetery in Fulton testifies that Sam lived fifty-six more years after the diary ended; she died November 6, 1919, at the age of eighty-five. We can reasonably assume from various records that she returned to Richmond sometime between Patty Curd's death in September 1863 and autumn of 1865. In the 1870 census, Francis Hart's Richmond household included: himself, Mary Curd, age 33, occupation "At Home," and Betty Hart, age 29, "Keeping House."[1] Richmond business directories listed her as living at her father's house at 210 W. Grace Street until his death in 1882. But after 1882, Sam disappeared from Richmond's standard historical records. The nature of these records makes it particularly difficult to trace the lives of women who were not attached to males.

Because financial and legal records of Tom Curd's estate are available, we do have rather extensive evidence of Sam's financial position after her husband's death. This evidence leads us to interesting speculations about Sam Curd's "place" in the world of business and property as the widow of a prosperous businessman. The degree of Tom Curd's prosperity is not entirely clear because of the nature of his business and his partnership with his brothers and other businessmen, but there are strong indications that he was a relatively wealthy man. In the 1860 census he listed the value of his real estate holdings at $30,000 and his personal property at $15,000. The inventory of Curd & Brothers' property (in which Tom Curd had an interest of "one equal undivided fourth") in May 1862 included: the contents of the dry goods store at $8,904.95; livestock (including "58 yearling mules") at $3,238.70; and the household goods at $178.50; for a total of $12,577.95 [sic]. (It is interesting to note that Tom and Sam's house and furniture were not owned by them, but by Curd & Brothers.) In addition, there were large amounts of property owned by Tom Curd and others and loans due to Curd & Brothers. One evaluation placed the value of the "notes and money" held by Curd and Brothers at $44,628.57.[2] When Sam finally settled with Isaac Curd for her share of the estate, extensive properties were listed in Missouri and Kansas.[3] Further, there are strong indications that there were additional properties in which Tom Curd had an interest, but which were never listed in the inventories, conveyances, or deeds of Tom Curd's estate. For instance, on March 25, 1864, the *Missouri Telegraph* announced a Sheriff's Sale at which the property of a Thomas Ansell would be sold as a result of "two executions, to me directed, both in favor of John Curd, administrator of the estate of Thomas Curd, deceased, and as such administrator, having in charge the partnership of Curd & Brothers. . . . " Of the plots named totaling 1900 acres, and of the twenty city lots in Fulton named in the announcement of the sheriff's sale, none appear elsewhere in the settlement of the estate, nor is there any indication that Sam received any payment for her interest in these properties.

In October 1865, M. S. Curd appointed Edwin Curd her attorney to sell lands to settle Tom Curd's estate. One year later she made a deed with Isaac Curd selling her interest in Tom Curd's estate for the sum of $7,000. Sam left the Curd family circle after the death of her husband and daughter with a payment of $7,000. We assume that her body was brought back to Fulton after her death, to rest under her tombstone in the family cemetery plot. These two acts—fifty-six years apart—speak clearly, if symbolically, of Sam Curd's place in the world.

The nineteenth-century division of labor and power between the sexes gave middleclass women an ideal role of wife, mother, and lady. As a "lady," a woman such as Sam became a symbol of her husband's status—her leisure and consumption (as Thorstein Veblen would write half a century later) became a sign of her husband's place in the world.[4] Middle class women, then, became more valuable the less their productive activity. Creating a "home" for Tom Curd meant providing a physical, peaceful, and moral haven away from the harsh competitive world of business. But as we have seen, Sam herself probably did few of the purposeful activities that provided the physical home. Instead, she was a symbol of her husband's status. When her husband died, her apparent usefulness ended, because her activities of consumption and leisure provided status for no one. It is interesting to note here that soon after Sam left Fulton to return to Richmond, Edwin, her only brother-in-law to do so, married.

The journal ends with a long description of Sam's feelings of depression: of loneliness and worthlessness as a widow and her inability to do anything to change the situation. Because she was unable to exert effort to control her situation, Sam assumed that it was God's will and that her role was not to murmur:

> Since I last wrote, time to *me* has not been measured by the brief span of days & weeks; but it has draged its *"weary length along"* with such heaviness, that I can scarcely be convinced that only 13 months have passed away since the death of my dear husband. Oh! God what hours of gloom & thick darkness, of lonliness bordering at times on despair, of weariness, feeling at night as if my days, had been of toil, & awakening with the same crushing consciousness, that I was *widowed*, a feeling which if language were exhausted no idea could be given of its full import. God & myself only know what I have felt to be—a *widow*. . . . Although 13 months have passed away, yet I feel my loneliness, my inestimable loss, my need of him, my indescribable bereavement, not to have abated, but increased, I feel that each day brings with it greater need of him. . . . I feel I need more grace to sustain me & I too often murmur at this Providence, would I could see it, & improve it as God intended it should be, for I know He will accomplish his design, & if this affliction be not improved he will come with some other. . . . I will write no more, for were I to fill this book, it would be but a repetition of sorrow's tale.

Sam's sense of loss was absolute—she had nothing to live for except her daughter Patty. Patty would also die five months later. Sam did not believe that she could live for herself—she lacked a sense of self for whom to live. What frequently began for nineteenth-century women as a commandment to make a home for others and to live for others—to nurture their husbands and children and to be the embodiment of selfless religious ideals—frequently became a repression of all feelings and expressions of individuality.

When Mary Jane Moffat and Charlotte Painter researched
women's diaries, they found that loneliness was the most common
emotion expressed by the diarists.[5] They attributed this loneliness
to women's inability to integrate both love and work into an au-
thentic self.

> When Freud was asked what the normal person should be
> able to do, he replied 'to love and to work.' We take this
> statement to mean that neither love nor work should obsess
> the individual to the exclusion of the other. From a healthy
> fusion of these two great human capacities will come power,
> not in the traditional sense of the word as ascendancy or con-
> trol over others but rather power as energy, emanating from
> the individual, a source of inner renewal that generates out-
> ward and returns to the individual.
>   We are familiar with the traditional cultural imbalance be-
> tween work and love, where women have been allowed au-
> thority only in the sphere of love while men attend to the
> work of the world. Such an imbalance results in a warped
> expression of the individual's potential energy. For women:
> self-pity, masochism, manipulation, celebration of the tor-
> ments of the heart, invalidism, madness. For men: slavery,
> war, corporate profits, destruction of the earth.[6]

Having no purposeful work, having always repressed her own
feelings, Sam Curd had no sense of her self. Throughout the diary
we see this in her constant loneliness: when she was in Fulton, she
longed to be with her Richmond family, but when she was in
Richmond, she longed to be with Mr. Curd. Having little consciousness of her own identity, she was emotionally alienated
from other people. Divorcing herself from her own feelings, particularly when those feelings were at variance with the cultural
ideal of the genteel and domestic female, she became absorbed
with the sentimental, melodramatic image of the person she
thought she should be. She was helpless in a world that she had no
power to control, and turned to self-pity and a complete abdication
of responsibility for her life to an omnipotent God who worked his
will, finally, by punishing.
    We sense that in the very act of keeping a diary Sam was at-
tempting to find some meaning in her life. The diary represents

her endeavor to integrate the disparate fragments, to resolve the
conflicts that she could not publicly acknowledge, in other words,
to find her self. Undoubtedly, there were additional reasons for
writing the diary. Like the account book that it actually was, the
diary was a listing of Sam's activities. Keeping a diary was a socially approved occupation; in his manual *The Young Husband* (1839),
William Alcott suggested that both husband and wife should keep
journals.[7] But there are many times when she used the diary to
express what could not be said publicly: her homesickness, her
southern sympathies, her unhappiness.

> I feel so terribly gloomy, this evening came thoughts in con-
> nection with the future almost overwhelm one, Oh! that I
> might become more reconciled to my *fate*. I feel as if I never
> could, I know it is wrong, I have so many blessings such as a
> good home, kind husband who is never ceasing in his good-
> ness to me, & the best of friends. Oh! that I might have the
> future in the hands of an all wise Creator, feeling that he will
> do best for me. All kinds of dark forbodings crowd into my
> mind this evening. I don't feel as it I could express my feelings
> to a mortal, & only write to try & find relief. (2/22/61)

Anaïs Nin and Tristine Ranier, who have used diary-writing as
a tool "for self-guidance and expanded creativity," recognize the
ability of diary-keeping to empower the diarist:

> We taught the diary as an exercise in creative will; as an exer-
> cise in synthesis; as a means to create a world according to
> our own wishes, not those of others; as a means of creating
> the self, of giving birth to ourselves. We taught diary writing
> as a way of reintegrating ourselves when experience shatters
> us, to help us out of the desperate loneliness of silence and
> the anxieties of alienation.[8]

In keeping a diary, Sam Curd may have been struggling to give
birth to her self. But against cultural forces that demanded that
she as a woman be self-less, that act was not enough. After her
husband's death, probably immediately before she wrote the long
final entry, Sam reread the diary and erased long passages. We can
only guess what these passages contained; perhaps she erased her

most self-assertive entries, judging them later to be disloyal or so antithetical to her public image, that they could not be allowed to exist. Symbolically, she was eradicating even this small vestige of her self.

Notes to Epilogue

1. *Richmond City and Henrico County, Virginia, United States Census*, Monroe Ward, p. 229, #21-23.

2. Callaway County Probate Court Records, Estate of Thomas Curd, 1862.

3. See Deed between Mary S. Curd and Isaac Curd, October 24, 1866, in Appendix E.

4. Veblen, *The Theory of the Leisure Class* (New York: Funk and Wagnalls, n.d.), pp. 130-146.

5. Mary Jane Moffat and Charlotte Painter (eds.), *Revelations: Diaries of Women* (New York: Vintage Books, 1974), p. 5.

6. *Ibid.*, p. 7.

7. From John S. Haller and Robin M. Haller, *Physician and Sexuality in Victorian America* (New York: W. W. Norton & Co., 1974), pp. 227-229.

8. Tristine Rainer, *The New Diary*, with a preface by Anaïs Nin (Los Angeles: J. P. Tarcher, Inc., 1978).

APPENDIX A

HART FAMILY GENEALOGY

Andrew Hart, b. 1754 (Scotland), d. 1832 (Virginia)
m. (1) Elizabeth Leake, 1786, d. 1792
  1. Mary, m. David Young
  2. Samuel Frances Leake Hart, m. Ann Taylor Curd, 1813. Moved to Fulton, Mo.; had eight children, including Laura Catherine Hart, m. George Edmund Otey Hockaday.

m. (2) Elizabeth Overton Bickley, 1793 (Elizabeth's sister was Martha Watkins, who married Samuel Dyer; they had at least eight children living in Fulton, Mo., including: Mary J. Nicholson, Martha Watkins, Sam Dyer, Virginia Lawther, and Sue Tuttle.)
  3. James, m. (1) Sophia Harris ⎱ lived at Fruitland, near
            (2) Francis Thomas ⎰ Keswick, Virginia
                Meriweather
  4. Andrew, a Presbyterian minister
  5. John B., a merchant, "but at length overtaken by commercial disaster, removed to Alexandria, where he died."
  6. Francis Bickley, b. 1802?, m. Martha Jane Dandridge, 1828, d. 1882
     i. Jane, b. 1830, m. Matthew Anderson?
     ii. Mary Samuella, b. 1834, m. Thomas Curd, 1860, d. 1919
     iii. Betty, b. 1840
     iv. Martha, b. 1849
  7. William D., a great success; he lived at the family estate of Sunny Bank; his only daughter Elizabeth ("Betsy") married Thomas R. Dew.
  8. Elizabeth, m. William B. Harris
  9. Margaret, m. Thornton Rogers
  10. Celia, m. Jacob Snider of Mississippi

From Rev. Edgar Woods, *Albemarle County in Virginia* (Charlottesville, Va.: Michie Co., 1901).

APPENDIX B

RICHMOND CITY AND HENRICO COUNTY, VIRGINIA, CENSUS

		Race	Sex	Age
1840:	F. B. Hart	1 W[hite]	M[ale]	30-40
		1 W	F[emale]	under 5
		2 W	F	5-10
		2 W	F	20-30
	slaves	2	M	under 10
		1	M	10-24
		1	F	10-24
		1	F	24-36

	Age	Sex	Birth Place	Date
1850: Hart, Francis B.	48	M	Va.	
Jane	20	F	"	
Mary	16	F	"	
Betty	10	F	"	
Martha	1	F	"	
Anderson, Matthew G.	27	M	"	

Richmond City and Henrico County, Virginia, United States Census, Compiled and Published by Virginia Genealogical Society.

APPENDIX C
CURD FAMILY GENEALOGY

Col. John Curd, b. 1751, d. 1819; m. Ann Underwood, b. 1747, d. 1826

1. Rebecca, b. 1779, m. Benjamin Anderson
2. Katherine, b. 1781, d. 1802
3. Isaac, b. 1783, d. 1850; m. Jane Watkins, b. 1789
    i. Katherine ("Kitty"), b. 1809, d. Glasgow, Mo., 1883; m. F. W. Digges
    ii. Ann Maria, b. 1813, d. young
    iii. Jane, b. 1815, d. unmarried
    iv. John, b. 1817, d. unmarried, 1865
    v. Thomas, b. 1823, d. 1862; m. Mary Samuella Hart, 1860
    vi. Isaac, b. 1826, d. unmarried, 1914
    vii. Edwin B., b. 1829, d. 1914; m. Harriet Webster, 1865
    viii. Harriet, d. young
    ix. Martha, d. young
    x. Martha Jane ("Matt"), b. 1833, lived in Colorado Springs, Col., d. 1923
4. Thomas, b. 1786, d. 1848; m. (1) Caroline Pleasants
                                    (2) Mrs. Jane (Lewis) Dandridge
5. Ann T., b. 1790, m. Samuel L. Hart; moved to Missouri and had eight children.

From Thomas H. S. Curd, Jr., *Supplement to the Curd Family in America* (Roanoke, Va., 1981). (Original text compiled by Frank D. Fuller and Thomas H. S. Curd, 1938.)

APPENDIX D
INVENTORY OF TOM CURD'S ESTATE:
HOUSEHOLD GOODS

1 Marble-top Table   5 Cushion Chairs
4 Rocking Chairs   1 What not   1 Sofa   2 lamps
Carpet & Stools   1 bureau   1 Bed Stead & beding
4 chairs   1 marble top wash Stand
1 Bowl & pitcher   1 clock   4 curtains
1 carpet   2 Shovel & tongs   1 Stair carpet
1 Wash Stand pitcher & bowl   1 Stove
3 Chairs   1 oil cloth carpet   What not & look glass
1 bedstead & bedding   1 lot bed clothing
1 Small stand   1 bed stead & bedding
1 bureau   1 stand   1 carpet   2 chairs
2 Curtains   12 split Chairs   2 Side boards
1 dining table   1 Stove   Cupboard & furniture
1 Castor   1 water jar & 2 pitchers
2 lamps   pr. candlesticks   oil carpeting
Cooking utensils   800 ″ bacon   Brick
Chicken coop   Kettle   Wheel barrow & Hoes
1 Bed Stead & Beding   lounge & Beding
1 Ward robe & Bureau   Carpet & stools
1 Rocking & 5 chairs   2 curtains
200 ft. plank

APPENDIX D
DEED BETWEEN MARY S. CURD AND ISAAC CURD, OCTOBER 1866

This deed made and entered into the 24th day of October 1866 by and betwen Mary S. Curd of the first part and Isaac Curd of Buchanan County Missouri of the second part. Witnesseth. That for and in consideration of the sum of seven thousand dollars to the party of the first part in hand paid the receipt of which is hereby acknowledged I the said Mary S. Curd have bargained granted and sold and by these presents do grant bargain and sell unto the said Isaac Curd all my right title and interest in and to the following described real Estate Situated in Buchanan County Missouri to wit lot No. 6 in Block No. 17 in Patris 1st (?) addition to the City of Saint Joseph lot No. 2 in Block No. 59 in original town now City of Saint Joseph lot No. 5 in Block No. 60 in original town now city of Saint Joseph lot No. 1 in Block No. 41 in Smiths Addition to the city of St. Joseph, thirty two acres of land lying in East Side of SE ¼ section of Township 57 Range 35, also sixty five acres of land in NE corner of SW ¼ of section 3 township 57 Range 35. Also West half of the East half of North West fourth of Section 32 township 57 Range 34. Also the South East fourth of section 19 Township 57 Range 34. Also twenty acres of land lying in the NorthEast corner of the North East fourth of Section 4 township 57 Range 35. Also the following real Estate situated in Doniphan County Kansas. To wit. The East half of and the North West fourth of addition 24 Township 3 Range 20. Also the North West fourth of Section 3 Township 4 Range 20. Also the North West fourth of Section 19 township 3 Range 21. Also the South half of section 23 township 3 Range 20. Also the East half of the North East fourth of Section 23 township 3 Range 20. Also the following Real Estate situated in Callaway County Missouri. To wit. lots X No. 195 and 196 in H. O. Hockaday's addition to the town of Fulton. Also a part of a lot beginning at the South West Corner of lot No. 196 in I. O. Hockaday's addition to Fulton running then at (?) 1¼° East along the West Side of said lot 3 chains South 1¼° then 3 chains and 17 links Then East to the beginning. Also part of lot No. 141 in the original town now city of Fulton, containing 22 feet front on Court Street running back 99 feet, being nearly West of the Court House and being the same ground on which is situated the Store

House heretofore occupied by Curd & Bros. and E. Curd & Bros.
and E. & I. Curd and now occupied by Hentley and Harris. Also
twenty feet to be taken off of lot No. 154 beginning on Jefferson
Street formerly Michals Street at the street corner of said lot then
running back an easterly direction 90 feet then at North 120 feet
thence West 90 feet then on south to the beginning. Also lots No.
11 and 12 in I. N. Hockaday addition to the town now city of Fulton. To have and to hold the aforesaid described real estate together with all and singular (?) privileges. And appurtenances
thereunto belonging or in any inso (?) appertaining unto him the
said Isaac Curd his heirs and assigns to forever. I also in (?) of the
same consideration sell and transfer all my right title and interest
in and to the following. Bank Stocks to wit. One hundred and one
shares in Western Bank of Missouri and Branch. Seventy Shares
in the Bank of the State of Missouri. And thirty nine shares of
Farmers and Mechanics Savings Institution at Saint Joseph Mo.
Also all my right title and interest in and to all notes and books.
And accounts that may be due owing and belonging to the late
firms of Curd & Bros., E. Curd & Bros. at Fulton Mo and I & T
Curd and I & J. Curd at Saint Joseph Missouri. Whether the same
be reduced to judgments or not. It is expressly understood that the
interest in and to said real Estate and personal property herein
described is the one undivided fourth part thereof and inheritance
as owned by me as follows to wit. My late husband Thomas Curd
was a member of said firms aforesaid and at his death he left a child
which has since died and through that child I as the mother inherit
the said one undivided one fourth part aforesaid. It is further and
expressly understood that I only carry my interest in and to said
property aforesaid both real and personal and which is subject to
all the debts of said firms and I am in no wise to be responsible for
the same or for the title thereof nor am I to be responsible should it
take the whole of said property to pay the debts of said firms
aforesaid.

Signed Mary S. Curd   City of Richmond Virginia

APPENDIX E
THOMAS CURD'S ESTATE: DOCTOR'S BILL

To R. Abbot Dr.

1861		
June 30	Croton oil Liniment Self	25
July 12	Visit wife & detention one day & night	5 00
13	Attention to wife	1 50
15	Visit wife obst. services & extra detention	10 00
Oct 9	[unreadable] self nettlerash	75
1862		
Feb 1	Visit self & med	1 25
2,4,5,6	4 days attention & med self	5 00
7,8,10,12	4 days attention & med self	5 00
"	bot Cod Liver Oil	1 00
13,14,15,16	4 days attention self & med	5 00
17	2 visits self & medicine	2 50
15,20,21,22	4 days attention self & med	5 00
26	visit visit self & med	1 25
Mar 1	visit self & med	1 25
6,15,20,21	4 days attention self & med	5 00
Apl 1	bot Cough mixt	75
3	prescription & tonic	75
9	6 oz Morphine solution	75
26	prescription self & med	75
28	night visit self at St. Aubert & atten thro day	10 00

$62.75

Bibliography

Arpad, Susan S. and Joseph J. Arpad. "Consciousness Changing in the Women's Studies Classroom," *Proceedings of the Conference on Communication, Language, and Sex*, Cynthia L. Berryman and Virginia A. Eman (eds.), Rowley, Mass.: Newbury House Publishers, 1980, 161-174.

Beard, Mary R. *Woman As Force In History*. New York: Mac Millan Publishing Co., Inc., 1946.

Bell, Ovid. *The First Presbyterian Church, Fulton, Missouri*. Privately published, 1948.

———. *Political Conditions in Callaway Before the Civil War Began*. Privately published, 1952.

———. *The Story of the Kingdom of Callaway*. Privately published, 1952.

Boylan, Anne M. "Evangelical Womanhood in the Nineteenth Century: The Role of Women in Sunday Schools," *Feminist Studies* IV, 3 (October 1978), 62-80.

Carrigan, Jo Ann. "Nineteenth Century Rural Self-Sufficiency," *Arkansas Historical Quarterly*, 21 (1962), 132-145.

Chesler, Phyllis. *Women & Madness*. New York: Avon Books, 1972.

Cott, Nancy F. *The Bonds of Womanhood: "Woman's Sphere" in New England, 1708-1835*. New Haven: Yale University Press, 1977.

Davidoff, Leonore. *The Best Circles: Women and Society in Victorian England*. Totowa, N.J.: Rowman and Littlefield, 1973.

De Beauvoir, Simone. *The Second Sex*. New York: Alfred A. Knopf, Inc., 1952.

Degler, Carl N. *At Odds: Women and the Family in America from the Revolution to the Present*. New York: Oxford University Press, 1980.

Diamond, Arlyn and Lee R. Edwards (eds.). *The Authority of Experience: Essays In Feminist Criticism.* Amherst: University of Massachusetts Press, 1977.

Douglas, Ann. *The Feminization of American Culture.* New York: Avon Books, 1977.

Du Bois, Ellen, Mari Jo Buhle, Temma Kaplan, Gerda Lerner, and Carroll Smith-Rosenberg. "Politics and Culture In Women's History: A Symposium," *Feminist Studies* VI, 1 (Spring 1980), 26-64.

Duffin, Lorna. "The Conspicuous Consumptive: Woman as an Invalid," *The Nineteenth-Century Woman: Her Cultural and Physical World.* Sara Delamont and Lorna Duffin (eds.). New York: Barnes & Noble Books, 1978.

Epstein, Barbara Leslie. *The Politics of Domesticity: Women, Evangelism, and Temperance in Nineteenth-Century America.* Middletown, Conn.: Wesleyan University Press, 1981.

Faragher, John Mack. "The Midwestern Farming Family, 1850," *Women's America: Refocusing the Past.* Linda K. Kerber and Jane De Hart Mathews (eds). New York: Oxford University Press, 1982.
_____. *Women and Men on the Overland Trail.* New Haven: Yale University Press, 1979.

Faragher, Johnny and Christine Stansell. "Women and Their Families on the Overland Trail to California and Oregon, 1842-1867," *Women's Experience in America: An Historical Anthology.* Esther Katz and Anita Rapone (eds.). New Brunswick, N.J.: Transaction Books, 1980.

Fisher, Christiane. *Let Them Speak for Themselves: Women in the American West, 1849-1900.* New York: E. P. Dutton, 1978.

Friedan, Betty. *The Feminine Mystique.* New York: Dell Publishing Co., Inc., 1963.

Fuller, Frank D. and Thomas H. S. Curd. *The Curd Family in America.* Rutland, Vermont: The Tuttle Publishing Company, Inc., 1938. Reprinted with supplement by Thomas H. S. Curd, Jr., Roanoke, Virginia, 1981.

Gluck, Sherna (ed.). *From Parlor to Prison: Five American Suffragists Talk About Their Lives.* New York: Vintage Books, 1976.

Gottschalk, Louis, Clyde Kluckhohn, and Robert Angell, *The Use of*

Personal Documents in History, Anthropology, and Sociology. New York: Social Science Research Council, n.d.

Haller, John S. and Robin M. Haller. *The Physician and Sexuality in Victorian America*. New York: W. W. Norton & Co., Inc., 1974.

Hampsten, Elizabeth. *Read This Only to Yourself: the Private Writings of Midwestern Women, 1880-1910*. Bloomington: Indiana University Press, 1982.

Hareven, Tamara K. "Family Time and Historical Time," *Daedalus*, 106 (Spring 1977), 57-70.

Hargreaves, Mary W. M. "Homesteading and Homemaking on the Plains: A Review," *Agricultural History*, XLVII, 2 (April 1973), 156-163.

———. "Women In the Agricultural Settlement of the Northern Plains," *Agricultural History*, L, 1 (January 1976), 179-189.

Harris, Ann Sutherland and Linda Nochlin. *Women Artists, 1550-1950*. New York: Alfred A. Knopf, 1979.

Harris, Barbara J. *Beyond Her Sphere: Women and the Professions in American History*. Westport, Conn.: Greenwood Press, 1978.

Hartley, Florence. *The Ladies' Book of Etiquette and Manual of Politeness*. Boston: G. W. Cottrell, Publisher, 1860.

Hiatt, Mary. *The Way Women Write*. New York: Columbia University, Teachers College Press, 1977.

History of Callaway County, Missouri. St. Louis: National Historical Company, 1884.

Hogeland, Ronald W. " 'The Female Appendage': Feminine Life Styles in America, 1820-1861," *Civil War History*, 17 (June 1971), 101-114.

Janeway, Elizabeth. *Man's World, Woman's Place: A Study in Social Mythology*. New York: Delta Books, 1971.

Jeffrey, Julie Roy. *Frontier Women: The Trans-Mississippi West 1840-1880*. New York: Hill and Wang, 1979.

Katz, Esther and Anita Rapone (eds.). *Women's Experience In America: An Historical Anthology*. New Brunswick, N.J.: Transaction Books, 1980.

Kaye, Frances W. "The Ladies' Department of the *Ohio Cultivator*, 1845-1855: A Feminist Forum," *Agricultural History* L, 2 (April 1976), 414-423.

Kennedy, David M. *Birth Control in America: The Career of Margaret Sanger.* New Haven: Yale University Press, 1970.

Kolbenschlag, Madonna. *Kiss Sleeping Beauty Goodbye: Breaking the Spell of Feminine Myths and Models.* Garden City, New York: Doubleday & Company, Inc., 1979.

Lerner, Gerda. *The Grimke Sisters from South Carolina: Pioneers for Women's Rights and Abolition.* New York: Schocken Books, 1971.

_____. "Placing Women in History: Definitions and Challenges," *Feminist Studies* III, 1/2 (Fall 1975).

Martine, Arthur. *Martine's Hand-Book of Etiquette.* New York: Dick & Fitzgerald, Publishers, 1865.

Matthews, William (comp.) with assistance of Roy Harvey Pearce. *American Diaries: An Annotated Bibliography of American Diaries Written Prior to the Year 1861.* Berkeley and Los Angeles: University of California Press, 1945.

McReynolds, Edwin C. *Missouri: A History of the Crossroads State.* Norman, Oklahoma: University of Oklahoma Press, 1962.

Miller, Jean Baker. *Toward A New Psychology of Women.* Boston: Beacon Press, 1976.

Modell, John and Tamara K. Hareven. "Urbanization and the Malleable Household: An Examination of Boarding and Lodging in American Families," *Journal of Marriage and the Family* (August 1973), 467-479.

Moffat, Mary Jane and Charlotte Painter (eds.). *Revelations: Diaries of Women.* New York: Vintage Books, 1975.

Motz, Marilyn Ferris. "Marking Time: Daily Journals of Nineteenth Century Rural Americans," a paper delivered at the Seventh American Studies Association Convention, 1979.

Parrish, William E. *A History of Missouri, 1860-1875,* Vol. III. Columbia: University of Missouri Press, 1973.

Porterfield, Amanda. *Feminine Spirituality in America, From Sarah Edwards to Martha Graham.* Philadelphia: Temple University Press, 1980.

Portrait and Biographical Record of Buchanan and Clinton Counties, Missouri. Chicago: Chapman Bros., 1893.

Ranier, Tristine. *The New Diary: How to Use a Journal for Self-Guidance*

170   BIBLIOGRAPHY

and Expanded Creativity. Los Angeles: J. P. Tarcher, Inc., 1978.

A Richmond Lady [Mrs. Sallie A. B. Putnam]. *Richmond During the War: Four Years of Personal Observation.* New York: G. W. Carleton & Co., Publishers, 1867.

Riley, Glenda. *Frontierswoman: The Iowa Experience.* Ames: The Iowa State University Press, 1981.

_____. "Images of the Frontierswoman: Iowa As A Case Study," *The Western Historical Quarterly* VIII, 2 (April 1977), 189-202.

_____. "The Subtle Subversion: Changes in the Traditionalist Image of the American Woman," *The Historian* XXXII, 2 (February 1970), 210-227.

Roberts, Helene. "Submission, Masochism and Narcissism: Three Aspects of Women's Role As Reflected In Dress," *Women's Lives: Perspectives on Progress and Change.* Virginia Lee Lussier and Joyce Jennings Walstedt (eds.). Newark, Del.: University of Delaware Press, 1977.

Rosenberg, Charles E. "Sexuality, Class and Role in 19th-Century America," *American Quarterly,* 25 (May 1973), 131-153.

Rowbotham, Sheila. *Woman's Consciousness, Man's World.* Harmondsworth, England: Penguin Books, 1973.

Ruoff, John C. "Frivolity to Consumption: Or Southern Women In Antebellum Literature," *Civil War History,* 18 (September 1972), 213-229.

Schlissel, Lillian. "Diaries of Frontier Women: On Learning to Read the Obscured Patterns," *Woman's Being, Woman's Place: Female Identity and Vocation in American History.* Mary Kelley (ed.). Boston: G. K. Hall & Co., 1979.

_____. *Women's Diaries of the Westward Journey.* New York: Schocken Books, 1982.

Schlesinger, Arthur M. *Learning How to Behave: A Historical Study of American Etiquette Books.* New York: The Mac Millan Company, 1947.

Scott, Anne Firor. *The Southern Lady, From Pedestal to Politics, 1830-1930.* Chicago: University of Chicago Press, 1970.

Sklar, Kathryn Kish. *Catharine Beecher: A Study in American Domesticity.* New York: W. W. Norton & Company, Inc., 1973.

Smith-Rosenberg, Carroll. "Beauty, the Beast and the Militant Woman: A Case Study in Sex Roles and Social Stress in Jacksonian America," *American Quarterly* XXIII, 4 (October 1971), 562-584.

_____"The Female World of Love and Ritual: Relations Between Women in Nineteenth-Century America," *Signs* I, 1 (Autumn 1975), 1-29.

_____. "The Hysterical Woman: Sex Roles and Role Conflict in Nineteenth Century America," *Social Research* XXXIX, 1 (Spring 1972), 652-678.

Snyder-Ott, Joelynn. "The Female Experience and Artistic Creativity," *Art Education*, XXVII, 6 (September 1974), 15-18.

Spacks, Patricia Meyer. *The Female Imagination*. New York: Alfred A. Knopf, 1975.

Stanley, Julia Penelope and Susan J. Wolfe (Robbins). "Toward a Feminist Aesthetic," *Chrysalis: A Magazine of Women's Culture*, 6, 57-71.

Stannard, David E. *The Puritan Way of Death: A Study in Religion, Culture, and Social Change*. Oxford: Oxford University Press, 1977.

Stoeltje, Beverly, J. "A Helpmate for Man Indeed": The Image of the Frontier Woman," *Journal of American Folklore*, LXXXVIII, 347 (January-March 1975), 25-41.

Stratton, Joanna L. *Pioneer Women: Voices from the Kansas Frontier*. New York: Simon and Schuster, 1981.

Tamke, Susan S. "Oral History and Popular Culture: A Method for the Study of the Experience of Culture," *Journal of Popular Culture* XI, 1 (Summer 1977), 267-279.

Taylor, Marjorie Caroline. "Domestic Arts and Crafts in Illinois (1800-1860)," *Journal of the Illinois State Historical Society*, (1940), 33.

Thomas, Emory M. *The Confederate State of Richmond: A Biography of the Capital*. Austin and London: University of Texas Press, 1971.

Thornwell, Emily. *The Lady's Guide to Perfect Gentility*. New York: Derby & Jackson, 1858.

Vander Velde, Lewis G. *The Presbyterian Churches and the Federal Union, 1861-1869*. Cambridge: Harvard University Press, 1932.

Veblen, Thorstein. *The Theory of the Leisure Class*. New York: Funk and Wagnalls, n.d.

Walters, Ronald G. (ed.). *Primers for Prudery: Sexual Advice to Victorian America*. Englewood Cliffs, N.J.: Prentice-Hall, Inc., 1974.

Weibel, Kathryn. *Mirror, Mirror: Images of Women Reflected in Popular Culture*. Garden City, N.Y.: Anchor Books, 1977.

Wellman, Judith. "Some Thoughts on the Psychohistorical Study
of Women," *The Psychohistory Review*, VII, 2 (Fall 1978), 20-24.

Welter, Barbara. "The Cult of True Womanhood: 1820-1860,"
American Quarterly 18 (Summer 1966), 151-174.

Woods, Rev. Edgar. *Albemarle County in Virginia*. Charlottesville,
Va.: Michie Co., 1901.